WHAT IT TAKES

WHAT IT TAKES

Good News from 100 of
America's Top Professional
and Business Women

Lee Gardenswartz, Ph.D.
Anita Rowe, Ph.D.

A Dolphin Book
Doubleday
New York
1987

To my mother, Rosyne,
and the memory of my father, Nathan, "Dempsey"
Always my wings and my anchor

To my other partner, Darrell
For encouraging me to be everything I can be
and loving the results

Library of Congress Cataloging-in-Publication Data

Gardenswartz, Lee.
  What it takes.

  "A Dolphin book."
  1. Success in business.   2. Personality and occupation.
3. Women in business—Interviews.   4. Women in the
professions—Interviews.   I. Rowe, Anita.   II. Title.
HF5386.G214   1987   650.1'024042   87-13657
ISBN 0-385-23820-7

CONTENTS

ACKNOWLEDGMENTS

This book belongs not only to us, but to the supportive and generous people who helped make it possible. We say thank you to:

The 100 incredible women whose experiences form the foundation of this book. We appreciate their time taken from busy schedules to talk with us. Their stories, so openly and honestly shared, are the grist for this mill.

Our agent, Barbara Lowenstein, who had the courage to bet on two unknown writers.

Our editor, Lisa Wager, whose skillful and astute editing was second only to her support and encouragement.

Tessa Warschaw, Ph.D., friend, colleague, and fellow writer, who unselfishly showed us the ropes. Her savvy advice has paid off.

Natasha Josefowitz, Ph.D., for being a sounding board at critical junctures in this project and for giving us insightful feedback.

John Jones, Ph.D., our mentor, role model, teacher, and friend, for helping us see the possibilities in ourselves and for enlarging our sights.

The Gardenswartz clan, the roots in my life from whose love I continue to be nourished—Beth, Art, Mark, Brenda, Ian, Marsha, Jill, Steve, Wesley, and Shira. They gave us their interest, suggestions, support, encouragement, and hospitality. They also gave us a band of miniature supporters in the form of nieces and nephews, especially Amy and Megan, who worked overtime scouting out prime locations for book signings. A very special thank you to Wesley and Shira who took time from finals and papers to read and reread various drafts of the manuscript. Their honest feedback was invaluable.

My (Lee's) Mom, "Ro," whose belief in us and this book never wavered. Her ability to balance undiluted cheerleading with helpful criticism was the ultimate support.

My (Anita's) parents, Marco and Petra Sabovich, who always encouraged my curiosity and achievement. Their love provided my solid foundation.

Ann Petty, Ph.D., reality-tester par excellence, whose quintessential comments helped make this a better book, and who believed in us even when we had our doubts. Her friendship and love are constant.

Darrell, "Bud," who loves us enough to tell us the truth even when it hurts, and who knew before we did what this book needed. He continues to keep us real and down to earth.

1
THE QUEST

"Lee-Lee, who told you that you could write this book?" A pretty insightful question from Lee's six-year-old niece. With the innocence that only a child can show, Megan's question got to the central issue of our book. Lee's answer, "No one told me I could but I'm doing it anyway," is at the heart of what we learned from interviewing 100 of America's top business and professional women. These women seemed to "have it all" . . . financial freedom, access to other movers and shakers, control in their own lives, satisfying relationships, and the ability to make their deepest dreams a reality. Like most women we know, we wanted what our interviewees had, but prior to this project, we didn't know what it took to get it.

What we learned from these super-achievers forms the basis of this book. The stories these 100 women tell are testimonies to the joy that comes from the abandonment of moderation. They show that the proverbial sky is the limit, that most people can do anything they want to. But there is a catch. Responsibility for making dreams come true rests squarely on the dreamer's shoulders. By stripping us of our excuses, the experiences of these women show us the potential power for success and joy in all of us.

We all see people full of potential who keep it locked in and bottled up. This is a book about unlocking and unbottling. We want it to empower you—to unleash your energy and ability so you can add your own definition to the "having it all" dictionary. This empowerment won't happen effortlessly or painlessly. Growth isn't that way. But with help, it's possible. We expect this book to serve as both a full-length mirror and a tool kit.

As a mirror, it will show you pictures of yourself. You will be pleased with some of what you see but you will also feel disquieted and experience a rumble in the gut. Good. Don't put the book down when you feel discomfort. Ride it through. By book's end, your rumble will have turned into a roar of confidence and power if you use the strategies that are part of the tool kit. By taking the risk to do some things differently, you can bring more joy, exhilaration, and prosperity to your life.

We've told you what this book is. What it is not is a book about becoming clones of the 100 women we interviewed. Nor does it advocate high level success in cookie cutter fashion. Rather, this book intends that you adapt what you learn from these women so that you may achieve the richness and satisfaction they have. Whether you are running a household or managing a department, raising kids or developing staff, completing a degree or beginning a new career, the lessons from the lives of these super-achievers can show you how to increase your joy and accomplishment.

LOOKING AT THE TOP OF THE LADDER
FROM THE BOTTOM RUNG

What prompted us to begin this quest was our own struggle for prosperity. In our evolution from teacher to entrepreneur we had come to believe that once you take charge of your own life, anything is possible. Having gone through one of the two major turnstiles open to women of our generation (being a ballerina was only a fantasy), we opted for teaching rather than nursing. Our first taste of independence came when we resigned from our secure jobs in the school district to start our own consulting business—still teaching—but in an adult, corporate environment. By presenting management seminars and running our own business, we became slaves to freedom.

The exhilaration we felt from making our own choices, breaking through limits, and controlling our own lives was addictive. While we liked running our own show, it wasn't always a bed of roses. In fact, the thorns were sometimes more apparent. Our business had survived the first four years, but it wasn't growing. We constantly compared ourselves with the women whose faces and stories graced the pages of *Savvy, Working Woman,* and the like. They ran their multimillion-dollar businesses from corner offices atop tall buildings, always with fresh flowers on their desks. They seemed to negotiate masterful, lucrative deals while wearing the latest designer clothes. We felt like Cinderella, being on the outside looking in. We knew no fairy godmother was going to wave her magic wand, though there were days we would have welcomed her.

The casualties of these constant comparisons? Dwindling self-esteem and growing self-doubt. We knew we had intelligence, skills, the appropriate letters after our names (Ph.D.'s in human behavior), and a track record of satisfied clients. But we also knew that those were not enough. We couldn't help wondering what these business tycoons had that we didn't.

GOING TO REAL LIFE LEGENDS
FOR THE ANSWERS

We had an inkling that our questions could not be answered in standard business school texts. We wanted to know how these successful women got to the top, what price they paid, whether it was worth the cost, and how we could achieve our own brand of success. For our answers we had to go to the "horse's mouth" and we decided to talk with thoroughbreds. We talked, face-to-face, with 100 of America's most successful business and professional women, who generously shared their stories and experiences. We interviewed the crème de la crème in their respective fields, women such as Shirley Hufstedler, first secretary of the Department of Education; Congress-woman Pat Schroeder of Colorado; Eileen Ford, co-owner of Ford Models, Inc.; Muriel Siebert, the first woman to hold a seat on the New York Stock Exchange; Mayor Dianne Feinstein of San Francisco; and Jane Evans, CEO of Monet Jewelers.

These success stories became our oracles. We didn't covet their positions, but we did want the kind of freedom, access, and control they have in their lives. Could their know-how show us the way? We thought so and we were not disappointed. The tapestry these women weave is rich. Their diversity makes for a brilliant kaleidoscope of skills, experiences, and contributions that teach and inspire.

Each individual defines success in her own way. Success is made up of a smorgasbord of facets, and depending on your perception, it might encompass any or all of the following elements: inner peace, wealth, satisfying personal relationships, fame, achievement (career or otherwise), and indepen-

dence. These are just a few of the many ways people character-
ize success. To make defining success even more difficult, these
words don't mean the same thing to everyone. How much
money is wealth? How much notoriety is fame? Is inner peace
the absence of conflict or does it require a transcendental feeling of calm? These few questions show that finding a single or
correct definition is impossible. But for this project we had to
identify a measurable set of criteria by which success would be
defined.

The women we interviewed met at least one of the following
criteria, markers of a certain kind of success which provide an
objective standard for the selection of interviewees:

1. CEO, president, or vice president of a large corporation or
   organization; chairman or vice chairman of the board
2. Entrepreneur with a business generating over $5 million
   worth of business per year
3. Public servant, elected or appointed to political office
4. Pioneer, a ground breaker in a particular field

Criteria established, we set about finding women who would
fit them. Our initial sources for interviewees were newspaper
and magazine articles about successful women. Once we began
the interview process, our population grew as a result of rec-
ommendations from the women with whom we had already
talked. Our group of interviewees is generously sprinkled with
members of the Committee of 200, a select group of America's
most successful businesswomen.

We sought diversity in both profession and location. Since it
was not feasible to interview all the women who fit our criteria,
we targeted major urban centers where we could get the highest concentration of women who did. A list of the women
interviewed and their demographics can be found in the Ap-
pendix. We utilized a series of questions to guide the interview.
These questions centered around the women's skills, values,

backgrounds, interests, and experiences. The data we collected are admittedly subjective—both on our part and theirs. Information was anecdotal and therefore hard to quantify, but what we saw and heard was so frequently repeated, it was hard to deny.

These 100 women are excessive in their behavior and inner driven. They have a compulsion to act, to put their energy into areas that are meaningful and enjoyable to them. They don't parcel out their energy, resources, or passion. They show this lust for life both at the office and at home. They stand out in a world of "wanters" because they abandon themselves to work that matters to them. They reap bountiful tangible rewards which are the indirect consequence of doing work they love. Their most striking feature is that they are less influenced by the approval or goals of others than they are by their own. The voice they listen to is the voice inside them.

DISPELLING THE MYTHS

Like most of you, we had preconceptions about what we'd find among women who appeared to have "made it." Many people are suspicious of success defined as "reaching the top" and have created a folklore about its down-side. This popular wisdom turned out to be popular myth. We quickly learned that many of the myths about successful women were just that. Those at the top have been given a bum rap. In our year and a half of interviews, the myths evaporated.

MYTH 1: Women Who Have Made It Are Queen Bees

Women who have achieved success in the male-dominated world bucked enormous odds. There is a prevailing thought that because they had to do it the hard way, they are not willing to make it easier for the women who follow. It is also thought that they are more competitive with other women than supportive.

We are not disputing the fact that there may be "queen bees," but we did not find this among the women we interviewed. Most make it a point to spend time, money, and energy helping other women. They counsel female professionals who seek their advice and form women's networking and support groups. They also align themselves with organizations that promote feminine strength. In our own project, they showed support and interest by rearranging schedules and opening doors to other interviewees.

Among them, there appear to be two schools of thought about helping other women. Some of our interviewees enjoy serving as mentors and feel a strong responsibility to hire and promote females. On the other hand, there are those who claim that the biggest compliment they can pay other women is to be gender free in decisions about mentoring, hiring, and promoting.

One of these, Chicago entrepreneur Sue Ling Gin, sees herself as a pioneer. She is pleased that her success has helped other women even though that was not her primary motive. She says, "I think all pioneers are alike. You knock down ten trees and you make it easier for others to come through. The purpose was to knock down ten trees, to get from point A to point B. It wasn't necessarily to motivate the troops behind you." Regardless of which side of the issue they are on, these role models are sensitive to the issues facing women in the work world.

Rather than feeling an innate competition with other women, they stressed their need for trusting, supportive relationships. They cherish friends with whom they can share similar problems, experiences, joys, frustrations, and challenges. Entertainment executive Ann Daniel tells a story that shows the kind of automatic connection and non-competitive relationship that she found with Barbara Corday, another inter-

viewee, when both worked for ABC, Ann in drama and Barbara in comedy.

Though they worked in the same company, they hardly
knew one another when they found themselves on the same
plane to Chicago. As Ann remembers, they began their conversation in Los Angeles and ended it when the wheels
touched down. Even though they hardly knew one another,
they got to a level of intimacy about important issues very
quickly. Ann realizes there is a danger that she and Barbara
may be chauvinistic, but she says, "We believe two men with
the little history we had would not have been able to get to the
basic level of exchange we did so quickly. The experience of
being female has such commonalities. There's a bond. The
same exists for men. Unfortunately for them, they learned a
different kind of bonding and their vulnerabilities are not valued." Bonding and open doors were what we saw, not competition and roadblocks.

MYTH 2: Successful Women Have Become More Like the Men than the Men Themselves

Common mythology holds that to make it in a man's world
women have to play the game like men do. That means deny-
ing their feminine, nurturing side to play hard ball. How is this
shown in the workplace? For starters, some believe women are
only accepted when they wear pinstripe suits with bow ties.
Further, they are listened to only when they are more logical
and analytical than intuitive, or when they pay more attention
to tasks than relationships. Wrong again. Over and over, our
interviewees highlighted the strengths they had as women. By
using their feminine skill as communicators and relationship
builders they got more accomplished. They used their intuition
to bring a new dimension to problem solving and they emphat-
ically stressed the contradiction of being in a woman's body
and trying to act like a man. They resisted the success uni-

form, insisting that they carve out their own styles. Utilizing the power in their femininity is a key strength.

MYTH 3: To Achieve a Position of Power, Women Have to Be Aggressive and Emasculating

Old-fashioned roles prescribe that a woman know her place. Society favors her when she is soft, demure, altruistic, and domestic. Women who act otherwise are sometimes considered aggressive and emasculating. It is believed that women who get to the top can do so only by being excessively pushy.

Among our 100, this is also a myth. These powerful women are definitely ambitious go-getters but there is a wide range of styles. While some are aggressive, far more are what CBS executive Ann Kalman terms "assertive with a velvet stick." This soft strength does the trick because they continue to be successful without leaving bleeding bodies or bruised male egos in their wakes. Their objective is not to be adversaries of men. However, their clarity and initiative may be perceived by some as combative.

As Hollywood model agent Nina Blanchard found out, the label is often in the eye of the beholder. In negotiating a contract for one of her clients, Nina was called "tough." That label didn't come from a chauvinistic male, but from a female producer who was also her friend. Surprised by her friend's comment, Nina asked, "Would you say that to a man who was negotiating for his client?" In fighting for the best contract, Nina was simply doing her job. Women don't always get kudos for that.

MYTH 4: Women at the Top Are One-Dimensional Workaholics

In order to get to the top, it is thought one must wear blinders and have an all-work-no-play life style. Another myth laid to rest. Myopia is not a disease we saw among successful women. To a person, they have more diverse activity and interests in their lives than anyone we know who has fewer responsibilities and demands on her time.

Besides the predictable interest in their businesses and tangential professional organizations, they showed an amazing breadth of involvement. From serving on foundation boards to campaigning for their favorite political causes, from savoring time with their families to ensuring time for the hobbies that rejuvenate them, their twenty-four-hour days have enough activity and variety of twice that many hours. The love affairs they have with their work don't keep them from engaging in a myriad of other interests. Part of what keeps them healthy and productive is this multiplicity.

MYTH 5: *Ambitious Strivers Sacrifice Everything for Success*

There was a time earlier in this century when women had to choose between career and family. The former required a huge sacrifice—giving up any vestiges of a "normal" life. Thankfully, this is no longer the case. That doesn't mean the juggling act for today's successful woman is easy. In fact, yesterday's career woman may have had it easier because choices were clearer and options more limited. Women today can have their cake and eat it too. The requirement is vigilant balancing of competing priorities.

The numbers show these women did not give up everything. Most are or have been married (85 percent) and have children (70 percent), and as we already mentioned, have multiple interests. Their lives are rich, full, and satisfying. Those who chose not to marry and/or have children did not feel they had sacrificed a complete life for success. They acknowledge, regardless of the paths they chose, that their lives aren't always easy. But then, whose life is?

MYTH 6: *It's Not What You Know but Who You Know (Or Are Related to)*

This commonly heard aphorism is applied to both successful men and women. Of the 100 women we talked to, only a few were related to their companies' founders. Even as daughters or wives, they wouldn't have increased profitability and made their businesses grow without skills and abilities in their own right.

Kathryn Klinger is an example of making a difference even with a connection. As president of Georgette Klinger Salons, founded by her mother, it might be easy to dismiss Kathryn's contributions to the organization. But they are significant. When Kathryn came to the helm, there were two salons, one in New York and one in Beverly Hills. Under Kathryn's leadership, there are now seven. Beyond increasing the number of salons, her customer base presently includes men. In addition, the salons have become full-service rather than just offering facials and makeup. Kathryn has expanded every aspect of the business, but the question of capability vs. connection remains. Judge for yourself. Is she riding on her mother's coattails? No matter how easily doors opened for her or others, contacts were not enough. Competence and initiative were critical factors in their success.

You're sure to have your own reactions to these myths. You may even have others you'd like to add to this list. But hanging on to them is not productive. It is important to look at them as myths, not realities, because believing them gives you excuses for not succeeding.

These women are living proof that anything is possible. Whether or not your dreams coincide with theirs, the fact that they've achieved their own means they have much to teach. We know what talking with these women has done to increase our feelings of power and effectiveness. We also know that their lessons can do the same for you provided your mind is open. We predict that everyone who reads this book, whether striving for the top or not, will get what she expects. Those who plan to learn how to increase their success, will. Those who skeptically argue with the book's message and simple truths will also make sure they are right. The result is yours for the taking.

2
LESSONS FROM THE LEGENDS: THE FIVE SUCCESS FACTORS

The most exciting part of our search is what we found. This chapter will explain the five factors common to these 100 women. You may be surprised to see that these are less skills and competencies than approaches to life and ways of looking at the world. Among such diverse personalities it was fascinating to find the echo of these themes getting stronger as we went from interview to interview.

These women are unique. They come from dissimilar backgrounds, have varied skills and experiences, grew up in different generations, and are products of various forms of education. Some are pro-ERA, some are anti. Some call themselves feminists, while others bristle at the label. Some are entrepreneurs who get high on running things themselves, while others thrive on the challenge of negotiating their way through the corporate power structure. Yet the lessons from their lives were amazingly the same. For example, take a look at Marilyn Lewis, founder and chairman of the board of Hamburger Hamlet Restaurants and Dianne Feinstein, mayor of San Francisco.

Marilyn, a dynamic and flamboyant ex-model, is not your

average chairman of the board. As a young woman, this fiery redhead hitched across the country to find fame and fortune as a fashion designer in the Big Orange. But fate had other plans for her. She fell in love with a young actor whose dream was to open an upscale hamburger joint. Together they formed a professional and personal partnership. What started as one Hollywood restaurant in 1950 is now a group of twenty-two across the country and the Lewises have been in hamburger heaven ever since.

Mayor Feinstein, on the other hand, is a cosmopolitan Stanford graduate raised in an affluent San Francisco family. To look at this poised woman, one might mistakenly assume that her life always went according to plan. In spite of her privileged upbringing, her childhood was not easy. Her picture-perfect family was ravaged by the erratic behavior of a mother with brain disease and her obstacles did not cease then. As an adult, she has dealt with the death of one spouse, divorce from another, and losses at the polls. Then, as a supervisor, she was thrust unexpectedly into the stewardship of San Francisco upon the murder of the previous mayor, George Mosconi. In her low key and controlled way, she has since earned the city's vote of confidence at the polls.

What would this politician who carves a path through the bureaucratic maze have in common with an entrepreneur who holds staff meetings poolside? A lot more than you'd think. These two women with vastly different styles are both highly successful and supremely effective at what they do. Marilyn's hamburger empire continues to grow and generates more than buns and pickles. It topped $30 million in 1984. The mayor, considered for the vice presidential spot on the Democratic ticket in 1984, is the highest vote getter in San Francisco's history. Employment is up, crime is down, and the treasury's cup runneth over. But that's just the beginning of their similarities. Scratch the surface of Marilyn and the mayor and you'll find two women who spend an inordinate amount of time thinking about their work. Excessive? Sure, but they love their jobs. They thrive on challenge and see new possibilities around every corner. They are undeterred by obstacles and problems. While they show their missionary zeal differently, work is their magnificent obsession.

They are only 2 of the 100 fascinating women who showed this paradox of core similarities contrasted with external differences. This contrast in styles, appearance, and professions made the sameness of their message even more powerful. The common threads stuck out like sore thumbs. From these 100 different personalities, five clear themes emerged. These women are *Four-Wheel Driven* and have a *Magnificent Obsession* about their work. They possess *Megavision* and a *No Excuses, Just Results* mentality. Finally, they perform *Practical Magic* in business with both people and numbers. The next section will give you a quick look at each of these factors.

1. FOUR-WHEEL DRIVEN

The most apparent quality these women possess is their compelling ambition. They are hard driving and hard charging. Much of their esteem rests on their achievements. Their self-starting mechanism comes as standard equipment. They don't know how to run any other way but in high gear. They move ahead full throttle, propelled by the four wheels of their drive—*Challenge, Change, Freedom, and Meaning*. These four wheels are the driving forces behind the motivation of all 100, but dominant drives differed and each personality is her own unique variation on a theme.

The *Challenge* to be the best has always driven Alexis Eliopulos, the only female manager of a five-star hotel in the country. Her drive propelled her from secretary to manager with a stint at every job in the hotel as she moved up. Once at the top, she took on the challenge of taking her hotel from a three-star rating to one of a few five-star hotels in the country in only two years. How did she do that?

When you enter the doors of L'Ermitage, an elegant European-style hotel tucked away in Beverly Hills, you begin to get the answer. You may see her inspecting every corner to give her hotel the white glove test. No detail is too small to go unnoticed. Though the hotel's accolades continue to pour in and its reputation is solid gold, Alexis refuses to rest on her laurels. She continues to strive for that non-existent six-star award because L'Ermitage aims to surpass the five-star rating it has already earned. A rare accomplishment and a rare woman.

Change is another of the *Four-Wheel Drives* and, in a world of people who resist it, Davina Lane, senior vice president of Cigna, a fast-growing health maintenance organization, is an anomoly. She can't tolerate boredom. When she starts feeling that way, she sits down with her boss and says, "I'm bored. I know how to do this. I've done a good job. Now I want to do something else." She sees this willingness to try something new, and to take responsibility for a project in which she may not be an expert, as one of her most important qualities. Davina puts her money where her mouth is. This ex-teacher now directs planning and construction of new facilities for Cigna. "My background isn't in construction but that doesn't mean I couldn't learn what had to be done. I'd never done a five-year plan before so I got a few books, read them, and decided which way to go. I'm not afraid to take a new challenge." Davina, like other *Change* cravers, does more than adapt to *Change*. She initiates it because she needs its variety and stimulation.

Lane Nemeth, true to her entrepreneurial nature, finds her drive rooted in *Freedom* and it goes back to childhood. She says, "I hated it [childhood]. Everyone tried to control me." Even then she knew who she was as a person and was smart enough to realize she had no power. That compulsion to control her own life led to her founding Discovery Toys eight years ago. "It's the first time I've been able to be my own boss, so it's the first time I've been able to be creative without having some boss say, 'You're threatening me. Stop.'"

Still others like Rabbi Laura Geller are driven by their need for *Meaning,* a desire to better the world around them. Rabbi Geller's quest for meaning took her from civil rights marches in the South to a kibbutz in Israel and ultimately to rabbinical school. The third woman rabbi ordained in the Reform movement, she currently serves as director of the University of Southern California Hillel Jewish Center.

Rabbi Geller explains her life's mission eloquently by referring to the first chapter of Genesis. "All human beings are created in the image of God. My task as a Jew and a Jewish leader is to create a world where all people can live as though they really are created in the image of God. Everything I do— whether it's interpersonal relationships or political organizing —in some way or another is shaped by that fundamental conviction on which my life depends." Whether spurred on by *Challenge, Change, Freedom, or Meaning,* all 100 super-achievers are excessively driven.

2. MAGNIFICENT OBSESSION

Energy, Joy, Hard Work, Intense Focus. These dynamic women bring their 1,000 watts of power and intensity to the work they love. The secret of their success is no secret. They are magnificently obsessed with businesses and professions they love passionately. They feel privileged to be so richly rewarded financially for work that is its own reward. The seven-day weeks and fourteen-hour days they usually put in replenish rather than exhaust them.

When Judge Joan Dempsey Klein enters a room, the force of her energy fills the space. But that energy is not frenetic. It

is harnessed and concentrated, whether she is on the tennis
court or the California Appellate Court. Like Justice Klein,
these women have the ability to block out distractions and
absorb themselves in whatever they are doing, whether at
home or at work.

They are immersed in their work because they love it. Carol
Sheppard, founder of Shop 'n Chek in Atlanta says of her early
years in business, "I was willing to sacrifice. I worked my butt
off—long hours, seven days a week." Judi Missett, the founder
of Jazzercise, put it in even plainer language. "Dream your
biggest, most terrific dreams. Then, work your ass off."

And work their asses off they do. But it isn't nose to the
grindstone drudgery. In fact, it doesn't even seem like work.
Ellen Sigal, owner of her own development company in Washington, D.C., can be found under her hard hat on the construction site before office hours every morning. This daily
"fix" is what starts her day off right. It's a highlight she
wouldn't miss. She loves to see magnificent buildings rise out
of cavities in the earth. She would agree with Marilyn Lewis,
founder and owner of Hamburger Hamlet Restaurants, who
advises, "If you don't have fun while you're exhausting yourself, you'd better get out." The adage, "There are no free
lunches," is repeatedly borne out. Being this passionate about
your work costs—in energy, time, and relationships. But the
return on their *Magnificent Obsessions* is not only success, but
joy and exhilaration as well.

3. MEGAVISION

When these women plot, plan, scheme, and dream, it's on a
grand scale. They see possibilities in epic proportions and they
have a belief in themselves to match. They also want to leave
their mark. As poets, they'd be writing epics, not jingles. As
360-degree visionaries, they see a myriad of possibilities in

each venture. Finally, they have a deeply rooted belief in themselves that allows them to act boldly and make their audacious dreams a reality. These three parts, *Grand Scale Thinking, 360-Degree Vision, and Chutzpah* are the essence of *Megavision.*

Try this dream on for size—transforming the way Americans eat. Sandy Gooch admits to this daring goal. As a result of a life-threatening illness caused by food allergies, she quit the teaching profession and started her own chain of markets. Mrs. Gooch's Natural Food Ranch Markets sell only natural foods, with no preservatives or additives. Not content just to have a profitable business, in her quest to change eating habits, she educates her consumers, both young and old. "If you love me, don't feed me junk," says a poster proudly displayed in her stores. Her programs for elementary school children get comments like, "I never knew that sugar could affect your body that badly," and "I found that healthy food isn't that bad." Having just opened her sixth store, Sandy is making inroads in sugar-addicted America as she continues to think and act on a grand scale.

A 360-degree visionary par excellence is Marilyn Barnewall, a consultant to some of the nation's largest banks. She learned the banking business as she worked her way up to vice president at United Bank of Denver. Marilyn has initiated the concept of private banking, a way to better serve banks' up-scale customers. She's even appeared before one of Paul Volcker's committees to present some of her ideas for bettering the economy. As if that weren't enough, she's embarking on a whole new business, creating calendars and cards based around the theme "Success is . . ." which is also the title of a book she currently has in the works. Marilyn's very active brain continues to find offshoots from each idea. She doesn't rest until she's taken her ideas as far as they can go. Then she's on to ten more.

Finally, for *Megavision* to bolster dream accomplishment, a third quality is required—*Chutzpah.* The sense of daring and boldness that can translate big vision into hard reality is what one of our interviewees displayed in her early days in retailing. Currently regional vice president of a large department store chain, she started working for the company years ago. After two years, she was attracted to management and when asked if she'd like to be a buyer, she said, "No, I don't want to be a buyer but I would like to be a store manager." The collective jaws of the all-male group dropped. One of them said, "You don't understand. Women aren't store managers." Her reply, "Why not?" She saw an opportunity and had the audacity to seek it out. This kind of vision and boldness has been a powerful factor in helping her and these women achieve their success.

4. NO EXCUSES, JUST RESULTS

This is where the rubber meets the road. Have these women met obstacles? Faced discrimination? Most definitely. Have they let it stop them? Absolutely not. No matter how high the hurdles, they manage to jump over them. They remain undaunted. Many commented that obstacles only served to spur them on.

This *No Excuses, Just Results* attitude is also found in a resilience that refuses to take no for an answer. Claire Rothman shows this results orientation. As vice president and general manager of the Forum, an 18,000-seat facility that is the home of the Lakers, she hosts some of the hottest names in entertainment. Claire books the likes of Prince, Neil Diamond, and Rod Stewart. In deals that involve large budgets and even larger egos, a problem solver like Claire is required.

Here's an example of Claire's problem solving at work. When the Eagles wanted fans coming up to the stage during concerts, Claire knew it was a fire hazard. But she found a way to keep the Eagles, their fans, and the fire marshals happy by creating the "Controlled Spontaneous Response." The first six rows were allowed to come to the stage while security guards stationed in the sixth row kept the rest of the audience seated. Her brilliantly simple plan, which gave the illusion of the audience coming forward, solved the problem, produced the desired results, and kept all parties happy.

"Can't" is absent from these women's vocabularies. Our heads are still spinning from the forceful response of Irene Cohen, president of her own personnel agency. "Can't? There is no can't." The "where there's a will, there's a way" philosophy is alive and well among them. They've staged sit-ins to get bank loans and jobs. They've courted clients for as long as eight years before they got their first "yes." Some have known poverty and even been on welfare, yet all have been undeterred in achieving their goals. Excessive perseverance keeps paying off. As Judith Sans, president of her own Atlanta cosmetic company so aptly says and lives, "You can do the impossible. It just takes a little longer."

5. PRACTICAL MAGIC

These business wizards work their magic with people and with budgets. But they don't use sleight of hand techniques. The magic is based on sound, sensible principles used toward purposeful ends. Practical magic is a fusion of business savvy, people skills, and the ability to learn from everything. It is a shrewdness that parlays experiences into possibilities and finds a way to position arguments to get the maximum following for ideas.

Witness Christie Hefner, whose business savvy and people skills took the ailing Playboy Enterprises from the red into the black in three years. When Playboy had a problem with their video programs, she needed help from the best minds in business to solve it. Getting a day from VIP's with demanding schedules would not be easy. Christie knew that something had to be in it for them beyond a trip to New York City and lunch at Playboy's offices. She cleverly put forth an offer they couldn't refuse. She told them they'd have the opportunity to meet and interact with other exceptional business minds, and they would get cutting-edge information on what was then an explosive new industry (video). Four out of five think-tankers said yes and the only no in the group had a schedule conflict that could not be changed.

Christie uses this same shrewd thinking in dealing with her employees. Playboy celebrated its thirtieth anniversary before it had made a financial turn-around. Long on good will but short on cash, Christie gave each employee thirty shares of Playboy Enterprises. The staff was delighted and everyone emerged a winner.

How do Christie and others like her develop their clever tactics? In a phrase, they are zealous learners and their learning defies tradition. They learn from books and they learn from life experiences. These women aren't just quick studies. They actively seek out opportunities for learning and they make the most of the ones that are presented to them.

Their reading is varied and whether it's biographies, histories, or professional journals, non-fiction topped their lists. They are voracious consumers of the printed word (if nothing else is available, a cereal box will do). Julia Thomas, chairman and CEO of Bobrow/Thomas Associates by her own admission did not even own a television until recently. She preferred "compulsive reading of a lot of magazines and non-fiction." Julia and her ninety-nine colleagues have an insatiable appetite for learning, extraordinary business acumen, and refined people skills that make it possible for them to weave magic regularly.

In varying degrees, these five success factors appeared a hundred times over. The experiences and stories these super-achievers relate show that they are *Four-Wheel Driven*. Their *Magnificent Obsession* consumes them with work they love while their *Megavision* creates infinite possibilities. Their lives are models of the *No Excuses, Just Results* and *Practical Magic* concepts they embody so fully. (To see how you stack up in these five areas, take the quiz at the end of the book.)

CHARACTERISTICS IN CONCERT . . . AND IN EXCESS

We all have parts of these characteristics but we are not running our own multimillion-dollar businesses. Neither do we have the access, freedom, or money these women have. Why not?

It is not enough to draw on *some* of these characteristics. These women have them all and they reinforce one another to create a resonant melody. Megavision would be only a pipe dream without the drive necessary to translate these dreams into reality. Having a No Excuses mentality will not help you build a business if you lack financial savvy and the ability to make contacts willing to help you out. You can be obsessed about a business you love but never see it reach its potential if you lack vision.

What's more, having all these characteristics in moderate amounts won't get all the success possible for you. These women have distinguished themselves because they are excessive. They are intemperate in their passion for what they do and in the joy they receive in return. Their immoderate drive and their breadth of vision propel them to success. Their unwillingness to take "no" for an answer and their exemplary business and people skills assure accomplishment of their goals. They have what it takes.

For those of us raised on the "all things in moderation" credo, living excessively may be a hard concept to swallow.

Yet this is the very quality that makes these extraordinary people more successful than millions of equally talented, competent women. The dynamos we interviewed do not play life right down the middle. What they have done is show us that there is little success without excess. Their lives encourage anyone who wants more out of life to be a little off center, to be lustful, to be passionate and excessive about any worthwhile pursuit. Whether raising children, working, volunteering, or running a multimillion-dollar business, these super-achievers hold nothing back. The result is joy and satisfaction.

Beyond fulfillment, there is integrity. Contrary to the myth that money and power corrupt, we found that affluence, integrity, and happiness can go hand in hand. Our interviewees are not mortgaging personal fulfillment for professional success. They have lives that are full and rich. They love their work passionately and they are compulsively driven to make their mark. They anticipate their accomplishments on a huge scale and reap the rewards of their imagination and hard work. They create possibilities, not limits, and they are shrewd with both people and numbers. These action-oriented, self-starters with their expansive vision and persevering initiative are consummate professionals. They have been able to make their dreams a reality. You can too. The next chapters will show you how.

3
FOUR-WHEEL DRIVEN

"There is no magic to success. Successful people are not necessarily more brilliant or more talented than others; but they likely work harder, are more driven, have vision, and set higher goals."

ELLEN FUTTER

CAN YOU IMAGINE . . .

A Russian history major with no background in architecture, finance, or real estate, building a development company that *Inc.* magazine identified as the number-one growth company of 1982?

A high school dropout building a multimillion-dollar business manufacturing children's clothes?

A young welfare mother of two, with a husband in prison, making herself one of the preeminent banking consultants in the country?

What made it possible for these women to achieve such high levels of success? Among other things, DRIVE.

The women in the three snapshots you've just glimpsed, like the other ninety-seven with whom we talked, have been known to willingly and enthusiastically work seven days a week, fourteen hours a day. What is the force behind this drive? As we listened to these women rhapsodize about their professions, it became apparent that they have an all-consuming need to achieve. Their compulsion to accomplish is *Four-Wheel Driven. Challenge, Change, Freedom,* and *Meaning* propel them. Some are mostly enticed by the *Challenge* of solving problems and testing their limits. Others are more driven to be *Free* from constraints and *Free* to do things their own way. There are also those who above all crave *Change* for the stimulation and variety it brings. And finally, some are primarily driven by the desire for *Meaning,* the need to make a significant contribution to their corner of the world. Regardless of what drives them, their desire to achieve is off the charts.

What makes their drive so much stronger than that of the average competent professional? Can anyone have this high powered drive? Can you achieve your own brand of success without it? These questions are the subject of this chapter. By seeing what drives these powerful women, you will discover what drives you. Equally important, when your drive loses power, you'll get some ideas about how to recharge it.

FROM WHENCE THE DRIVE?

What drives people has been the subject of great thinkers for years. Teachers, parents, and managers all wonder why some people are driven to expect the best from themselves and some are not. There is no simple answer to this question. Abraham H. Maslow, a giant in the field of humanistic psychology, addressed the question of drive and motivation extensively. He saw all human behavior as motivated by universal needs: the need for psychological and physical safety and security; love and belonging; esteem; and the fulfillment of potential. Drive arises out of our attempt to satisfy these needs. Fulfilled needs don't motivate, unmet ones do.

Individuals attempt to meet their basic needs in different ways. These 100 successful women meet their needs for esteem and the fulfillment of potential by overcoming *Challenges,* initiating *Change,* seizing the *Freedom* to control their own lives and making a *Meaningful* contribution to the world. They are willing to work seventy-plus-hour weeks with lust and determination because that is how these two basic needs are met. Among the spirited women we interviewed, motivation comes from satisfying an internal need rather than getting an external reward. The doing is more important than the getting. Projects, tasks, and goals are rewards in and of themselves. While these accomplished women do not shun the tangible benefits of success that come to them, (in fact, they thoroughly enjoy the wealth, access, and other rewards they've accrued), those advantages are less influential in driving them than the pursuit and attainment of their own dreams.

They have chosen to put their esteem and fulfillment "eggs" in the work basket. It is possible to get those same needs for self-worth met by winning a golf tournament, running a marathon, or becoming a virtuoso. While we talked with women who get great pleasure out of golfing, running, and playing an instrument, those are not their primary sources of self-esteem. Work is. The success they feel in the work arena validates them daily. It also drives them.

Observing these women and comparing them with ourselves and others we know has raised some complex issues. People are not equally driven. What's more, it seems that drive is largely innate. Is this bad news for the person whose get up and go, got up and went? It depends. The key question for you is, DO YOU HAVE SUFFICIENT DRIVE TO ACCOM-

PLISH WHAT YOU WANT IN LIFE? If you do, pat yourself on the back and prop your feet up while you enjoy reading
this chapter. You can look at the drive of our interviewees and
get a different perspective on your own.

If, like most people, your list of wants is longer than your
track record of accomplishments, read on. You'll get some
ideas for boosting your drive. What's more, if the person
whose drive you are concerned about is your spouse, child,
subordinate, or other work associate, you have a lot of company. People wanting to infuse others with drive could, hand
in hand, circle the globe several times. If this description fits
you, we aren't going to show you how to "fix" these people.
No one can do that. But you will get some understanding
about drive that will help you in your dealings with those
under whom you'd like to light a fire. Let's start by understanding the four wheels behind drive.

CHALLENGE

Challenge, the first wheel of the drive, is the breakfast of
champions. It's the fuel food for these women and they eat it,
not just for breakfast, but for lunch and dinner as well. It
exhilarates and stimulates them. It draws them like a moth to
a flame, but unlike the flame, it not destructive.

The *Challenge* drive is three-pronged. For some women, the
Challenge is competition. They are driven to be the best. For
others, going beyond their own limits and proving themselves
gets their juices going. And lastly, there is the *Challenge* of
transformation. Converting an obstacle into an opportunity or
creating a solution for a problem is the name of the game, not
at all a trivial pursuit.

The Challenge of Competition

Hertz and Avis. NBC and CBS. Coke and Pepsi. What do they have in common? As fierce competitors, they are driven to be first in their fields. Many of the super-achievers we interviewed are driven by competition, too.

Competition has driven Mary Kay Ash, the creator of Mary Kay Cosmetics, since she was a child. This successful business-woman says the competitive spirit has served her well and she wishes more women would use it. Boys learn it early from sports; she learned it in a different way. This feminine version of Horatio Alger traces her competitiveness back to her friendship with Dorothy Zapp when they were seven years old.

Though they were good friends, they came from opposite sides of the financial tracks in their little Texas town. Mary Kay tells how every morning she'd walk around the corner and go to "fairyland" where Dorothy lived. Dorothy, in her freshly starched pinafore, had her golden curls arranged in a way that Mary Kay, with her bowl haircut, hungered for. That's not all Mary Kay hungered for. She ate the breakfast every morning that finicky Dorothy didn't want. There were other fringe benefits of being Dorothy's friend, such as going on vacation with Dorothy's family. Even at seven, Mary Kay knew that being a model of behavior would produce results. It was how she got strawberries with milk. It was also what made her feel equal to Dorothy as a person even though she wasn't equal financially. "Whatever Dorothy did, I had to do better. If Dorothy made an A, I had to make an A+. That was the competitiveness that started early and she was a great factor in my belief system."

The competitive zeal that Mary Kay experienced at seven is at the heart of her business today. Every month's issue of her consultant's magazine is filled with new contests and prizes. The *pièce de résistance* for her beauty consultants is the frequently joked about pink Cadillac. "What color was the car your company gave you?" quips Mary Kay, as she and her top saleswomen laugh all the way to the bank.

That need to be the best was expressed repeatedly among the women with whom we talked. Because the bywords of the 1980s are collaboration and cooperation, it has become fashionable in some quarters to knock the competitive spirit. Mary Kay exemplifies the fact that competition is not only alive and well but it can be positive and fruitful. It certainly has been for her and for another extraordinary woman, Judi Missett, whose drive was born early, too.

Judi is a natural dancer, performer, and teacher. This powerhouse whose creativity, sweat, and sinew gave birth to Jazzercise is a born competitor. Consider Judi at age eight. Her competitive drive was remarkable even then. Already a veteran of dance contests, she went to South Dakota for a dance championship at a local Czech Days celebration. Her dramatic, lyrical routine, though excellent, won her second place. Not good enough for Judi. She told her mother she was going back the next year to win first place. With a determination fueled by her intense desire to win, she figured out what was needed. Even at that young age, she was smart enough to see that no matter how well she danced, her graceful routine would never win a blue ribbon in that "um-pah-pah," polka-loving community. The following year, she created a flamboyant number that was right up their alley, complete with tap shoes, drums, and acrobatics. Judi made good on her promise, stole the show, and won the grand prize.

Judi is still competing. Now her rivals are Jane Fonda's Workout and Jackie Sorensen's Aerobic Dancing. She aims at making Jazzercise the biggest exercise program in the world. In fourteen years it has grown to 400,000 participants in the United States and fifteen other countries. Judi is exhilarated by competition, but that's not the only thing that drives her or these other women.

The Challenge of Testing Limits

"Successful people are willing to do things other people won't."

SALLY BEHN

Breaking through barriers is a *Challenge* all its own. It is rooted in our need to prove ourselves. Whether this need comes out of a desire to validate an already high self-esteem or a need to bolster an inadequate one, the drive it produces is the same. The women we interviewed showed both sources of that drive. For example, some interviewees talked about feeling unattractive as adolescents so they developed strengths in other areas to make up for their lack in the appearance department. Others didn't perceive inadequacies, they just became exhilarated when they tried new things and succeeded. They were addicted to pushing their own boundaries.

Irene Cohen showed us how this was true for her. She wanted to start her own business and make money at it—big money. When she told her husband that she wanted to leave personnel counseling and open her own employment agency, he was skeptical at best. Irene told him, "Look, you've had a chance to fail. I never have." She'd never know how far she could go if she didn't take that risk.

She got her chance but she didn't fail. Irene Cohen Personnel Services is a flourishing firm that now has three sibling companies. And her husband is now a believer who has joined the four-company enterprise. Irene continues to test her limits. When we talked with her, she had recently completed a crash course for small business in finance and business management at Stanford. Pretty challenging for someone with no college degree. These driven dynamos continually strive to meet *Challenges* because that's what makes them feel good about themselves.

Another person bitten by the limit-testing bug is Julia
Walsh, Washington, D.C., "super-broker" and currently managing director of Julia M. Walsh and Sons/Tucker Anthony
and R. L. Day. Her go-getter attitude paid off when she was
widowed in 1957. At that time this young mother became the
sole breadwinner for herself and her four young sons. Taking a
job at Ferris and Co., a Washington, D.C., stock brokerage,
she set about to prove herself in this arena. And prove herself
she did. By 1966 she was earning an annual commission of
$250,000 on sales to non-institutional accounts. As if being
one of the nation's top security sales people wasn't enough
proof of her capability, she found other ways to distinguish
herself. Julia's career is a case study in firsts. She was the first
woman to graduate from Harvard Business School's Advanced
Management Program in 1962, the first woman member of the
American Stock Exchange in 1970, and the first female repre-
sentative of the securities industry to serve on the Amex Board
of Governors in 1972. In stretching her limits, she expanded
the boundaries of others' perceptions about women's capabili-
ties.

Accomplishing all this and even the vice chairmanship of
Ferris and Co. was not enough for Julia. After twenty-two
years of success, it was time to push limits again. Julia, who by
now was remarried and the mother of twelve children (four by
her first husband, a daughter by her second, and seven step-
children), created a new challenge. In 1977 she started her
own brokerage firm, Julia M. Walsh and Sons. Her need to test
herself comes through when she says, "I wanted to build
something of my own, something I could get my teeth into.
Something that made me want to take the risk and go for the
brass ring." Julia admits she had a curiosity about whether or
not starting a successful business, and building financial security for herself and her family, could be done by a woman. The
answer in her case was a resounding "yes" as she and many of
her children work together to make her brokerage, recently

acquired by Tucker Anthony, and R. L. Day, a growing concern. Testing limits can serve you well, too. Think about times when you broke through some formidable barriers. If one of your feelings was exhilaration, did it make you want to go back for more? If so, the *Challenge* of testing limits drives you, too. Are you tapping that internal source of motivation? It could be a prime mover for you.

The Challenge of Transformation

There is yet another part to the *Challenge* drive. It's the Henry Higgins in all of us that wants to transform. Whether it's fixing organizations or people, the *Challenge* is to make something better. In her own "My Fair Lady" way, Nina Blanchard does that with models. For her the *Challenge* is taking young unknowns and making them stars. She's batted 1,000 with Christie Brinkley, Christina Ferrare, and Cheryl Tiegs, to name a few. While Nina gets her kicks from making stars out of people, Jane Hurd gets hers from doing makeovers of organizations.

How about this for fun—taking a job as CEO of a hospital that was $16.5 million in debt? To make it even more fun, look around the industry. Drastic cutbacks and budget restrictions abound as hospitals try to weather the changes in the health care field. Not what most people would consider a good time, but Jane Hurd jumped at the chance. With the help of her staff, she put Children's Hospital of Los Angeles in the black in eighteen months. For Jane, this is only the beginning. She has embarked on a massive building campaign. She is joint-venturing with physicians in private practice. She continues to attract top researchers to increase the institution's reputation. All this transformation is not without cost. It has meant constant change, cutbacks, and even layoffs. But Jane is driven to make Children's Hospital one of the preeminent health care facilities in the nation. This *Challenge* is what keeps boredom at bay and Jane on the job.

Whether it's competing to be the best and pushing yourself to new highs, testing limits, or transforming the world around you, *Challenge* is a powerful drive for all of the women with whom we talked. What part of the *Challenge* drive propels you? If it's competition, don't apologize, just do your best to win. If it's testing limits, keep pushing yourself to expand those boundaries. If it's transformation, change something that matters. Just remember that *Challenge* plays a critical role in drive. Use it and feel exhilarated.

CHANGE

"We know for sure that life is about change. Viewed this way, it *[Change]* is acceptable and inevitable. If we get hooked on the process not the structure, then we can have fun."

SANDY GOOCH

"When I get bored, I just start a new company." So says Henrietta Holsman, who has obviously been bored a few times. She presently heads four different companies on the West Coast, the chief one of which is Stockton Wire. Another interviewee, Julia Thomas, jokes that she needs so much *Change* that she's not happy unless she's in escrow. And a third, Mary Baim, president of Plywood Minnesota of Illinois, says, "I work for the thrill of change." This voracious appetite for *Change* they exemplify is the second wheel of the drive and another of the qualities that sets many of these driven professionals apart.

Most human beings resist *Change*. The desire for predictability and the security of the known overcome their need for stimulation and variety. The *Change* seekers we interviewed are different. They embrace *Change* because they understand it is necessary for growth and because they need the invigoration and *Challenge* it brings. It forces them to test themselves, to pit their skills and resources against various opponents. They welcome *Change* when it is inevitable and even more frequently, they initiate it. In this massive chess game called life, they have no intention of becoming pawns.

How do *Change* seekers like Henrietta, Julia and Mary manage to maintain stability in the face of continuous movement? We got an insightful clue from Tish Nettleship, the CEO of North Pacific Construction Management (NPCM), in Santa Monica. When an employee first suggested that Tish "liked change for change's sake," she was perplexed and astounded. Compulsive about organization and detail, Tish's first instinct was to see change as a disruption of order and the opposite of what she was striving to create. Since then, Tish has come to realize that the employee's remark was an entirely appropriate comment for her creative style at work, and equally inappropriate for her style at home.

Tish instinctively balances her need for *Change* with solid anchoring at home. Here's what she does. Before she moves into a residence, she diagrams on graph paper where everything goes. Within ten days of moving in, everything is in place from closets with clothing organized by weight and color to alphabetized spice racks. After that, "It never moves an inch. It's fixed." In the office, it's a very different story. They move offices and the equipment within them so frequently that NPCM staff jokes that they have permanent furniture movers on staff. Tish acknowledges this dichotomy when she says that the stability at home balances her change-seeking at work.

Like all *Change* seekers, lawyer turned entrepreneur Susan Bird is a self-proclaimed "adrenalin junkie." *Change* energizes her. She advises, "Be excessive. Forget about moderation. Embrace change."

Susan sees life as a continuum, a series of stages. She embraces *Change* because it thrusts her to the next level. By seeing her development that way she is able to "have it all." At one point, law school was top priority, at another, getting married and starting a family was. At this point her professional life takes center stage. Looking at life in phases means each decision is not the be all and end all. This view gives Susan a greater comfort with the risks involved in *Change*. It also provides answers to some hard questions women are asking.

In our seminars for professional women we constantly come face to face with women confronting critical dilemmas. Should I go back to school? If I do, what will it mean to my family? Should I take time from a burgeoning career to start a family? What will it cost me if I do . . . and if I don't? Should I take that promotion or new job if it means uprooting my family? No one but you has your answers to these tough questions. However, we believe Susan Bird's theory offers guidance and perspective to these gut-wrenching issues.

If you don't like *Change,* you may never be driven by it. But there is no way to avoid dealing with it. The old adage that it is the one constant is still true. The trick is to make *Change* your ally, not your enemy. Start enjoying the stimulation it brings by getting more comfortable with the process of *Change* through taking some low stakes risks. Here are a couple of examples that may impact your "comfortable old shoe" routines that put you on automatic pilot.

Become more comfortable with the change process by altering a small but noticeable appearance detail. Try a new hairdo or new nail polish. Exchange your bow tie for a scarf. These non-threatening *Changes* will demonstrate that you can survive *Change* and maybe even enjoy it.

Assess your morning ritual, the one you stumble through without a conscious thought. We know you like it—that's why it's become your ritual—but it's time to shake things up a bit. Read the morning paper after you exercise instead of before (or vice versa.) If you never eat breakfast, give yourself ten or fifteen minutes to enjoy a glass of juice, a piece of fruit, or a lingering cup of coffee with a stimulating morning read. Vary the route you take to work. Whether it's freeways, subways, or byways, there's always more than one way to skin a cat. A new route will spray a fresh coat of paint on an old, familiar destination.

Speaking of old and familiar, what is your tried and true restaurant hangout when you want reliable service and good food? We suggest you broaden that repertoire as well. Instead of going to the same Italian restaurant every Saturday night, try another kind of cuisine. This doesn't mean never frequenting a place you genuinely enjoy. But if you can enjoy one hangout, you can enjoy two or more.

Once you have disturbed your old habits and lived through (maybe even enjoyed?) some new ones, it's time to up the ante a little. Take on a new project at work or in an organization you belong to. If you've always avoided chairing a committee or holding an office, now's your chance. Make *Changes* in your own life as well as in your community by volunteering some of your time at an organization that reflects your aspirations and values for a better society.

You'll be ready for the "big leagues" of *Change* once you have mastered the "farm teams." Consider leaving that secure nest for the city of your dreams that has always tantalized you. Revise your resumé for a professional move or find out how to write a business plan so that you can successfully launch your own business. The variety and stimulation of *Change* can seduce you. Give it a chance.

FREEDOM

Freedom—exhilarating, intoxicating, seductive, and for many of our interviewees, absolutely imperative. The drive for *Freedom* is a powerful force that motivates these women. It is as basic as breathing and about as little noticed—except when they can't have it. For them, the lack of *Freedom* and control in their lives is suffocating.

It is not surprising that Frank Sinatra's recording, "I Did It My Way" hit such a responsive chord. Heroes, both mythical and real, are those who, against all odds, do it "their own way." These twentieth-century heroines savor the *Freedom* that taking control gives them, both to get what they want and to avoid what they don't. For many, that was poverty.

Freedom from Poverty

If you doubt the strength of the drive to be free from financial limits you need only to see the number of get-rich-quick schemes that attract people by the millions. From pork bellies and lottery mania to pyramid schemes and real estate, there is no shortage of ways to tantalize people with the dream of financial *Freedom*.

For those who grew up poor, the drive is even stronger. Depression-era poverty forged Shirley Hufstedler's drive. That's a good part of what accounts for her accomplishments. Landing a seat on the ninth Circuit Court of Appeals and a cabinet post are no small feats for anyone, but for a woman who went to law school in the 1940s, they are nothing short of miraculous.

Shirley has a keen intellect and incisive mind but those wouldn't have been enough without the drive that was formed early. As a child of the Depression, she went to work at age thirteen in a dime store where she earned twenty-five cents an hour. So did the women she worked with who raised families on their earnings. She watched them walk ten miles to save ten cents carfare. She made up her mind to have a different destiny. "I never called myself broke or poor. Mind you, I didn't have money. A combination of fear and ambition drove me. I made up my mind I would not live like that again ever ever ever." And she hasn't.

Judith Sans would understand Shirley's fear of poverty. She was driven by it, too. As president of her own cosmetic company in Atlanta, this woman who looks fifteen years younger than her mid-fifties age, is the best testimony for her products. She, too, was a wanter in a have-not world. Her Hungarian immigrant mother worked hard to make ends meet, but Judith and her sister wanted more than their mother could provide. The difference between the two siblings was that Judith was willing to do something about it. While her sister would sit home crying about the things she couldn't have, Judith was going to school and holding down three jobs. As a teenager, she fibbed about her age to get a job in a candy store, worked in an office, and then took sewing home for extra cash. These non-lucrative jobs were not precursors to Judith's present wealth, but the hard work and determination were. So was her drive. How many teenagers do you know who hold down three jobs at once?

It is no coincidence that so many of the highly achieving women we talked with have vivid memories of the Depression. That experience left them with a strong work ethic that involves long hours, hard work, and dues paying. Their drive was critical to lifting them out of poverty. This is in stark contrast to the popular baby boom expectation of a quick rise to the top, immediate gratification, and meteoric success. To the "boomers," the Depression is a history lesson while a high salary is considered an inalienable right. Today's professional woman has fewer obstacles than her predecessor, but she also has more competition, making drive just as critical for her as her Depression-era counterpart. Though circumstances and times have changed, the desire to achieve and be successful hasn't. When talent and skill are equal, the blue ribbon still goes to the most driven.

Freedom from Control

How do you react when you're told what to do? Many of the women we talked to start their own companies. They demonstrate the entrepreneurial spirit fueled by the drive for *Freedom* from control. While we have yet to meet the human being who doesn't want to move her own pieces on the chessboard of life, the drive for *Freedom* from control is much more pronounced among the entrepreneurs we interviewed. It is that specific desire for *Freedom* that got them to start their own businesses in the first place.

Ruth Scharf is a prime example. She was the child of immigrant parents. Tired of getting hand-me-downs as the middle of five girls, she quit high school to work so she could buy clothes. Ruth's spunk comes through when she talks about an experience in her early dating years. She and her boyfriend had stopped for something to eat. When Ruth ordered raw onion on her hamburger, he gave her the critical ultimatum. If Ruth gained an onion, she would lose a boyfriend. Do we need tell you what she chose? Even before the age of women's liberation, making her own decisions and taking control in her life was critical. From starting a business to deciding what to eat, Ruth wasn't going to be told what to do. That's why in her mid-forties she started her own company, Ruth Scharf, Ltd., a line of children's clothes.

Her original plans included two male partners. Smart thinking in the early sixties—partnering with men would make securing loans and other aspects of starting a new business easier. At the last minute, both men defaulted when they got offers they "couldn't refuse." They asked Ruth to wait until they were available. But spunky Ruth was through having her dreams depend on other people. She had already quit her job and knew if she didn't start her business then, she'd never do it.

In this age of the small business boom, mid-eighties style, her accomplishment could seem ho-hum. But twenty years ago when the likes of Lindas Gray and Evans were not showing us forty was wonderful, it was as close to over the hill as you could come without actually falling over the precipice. It certainly was not considered appropriate to start a new business at that stage of life. And a woman no less? Neither bankers nor jealous friends were encouraging. But that didn't matter. Ruth's drive was indomitable and it paid off. In 1984, she was listed in *Savvy*'s top sixty, an elite group of the top companies run by women. Since then, Ruth has sold her company to pursue another of her loves—selling antiques.

Control is harder to come by in corporations because being a company person is the expectation. As you think about your own career moves, consider this drive. If your appetite for *Freedom* is voracious, recognize that you run the risk of a nagging hunger unless you own your own company. A corporate structure does not lend itself to the kind of *Freedom* possible in entrepreneurial ventures.

As an organization woman or an entrepreneur, do you TAKE the *Freedom* to do what you want in your life? If not, are you bothered by a lack of autonomy? Where are you willing to begin exercising more control? Do you need to confront your boss? Are you feeling trapped in a dead end job? Do you tell yourself and others that you are staying because: 1. I have so much vested in the retirement system, 2. I don't know if I could get the same pay elsewhere, 3. I have to put my kids through college, or 4. All of the above? If you can answer yes to any of these four, you've just become a member of the Victim Club, a group that would be better off with zero membership. The dues come at a high price—control of your own life. There is a never-ending list of excuses for people staying in situations or relationships they don't like. But the result is always the same—a loss of vitality, hope, and initiative. By taking control, you can stop the drive drain.

We offer two caveats where the subject of control in your own life is concerned. First, attempting to control others is not a way to free yourself. It will only boomerang. Those you try to control have as much desire for *Freedom* as you do. The paradox is that the more you feel free and in charge of your own life, the less you will need to control the lives of others. The second caveat is that maintaining too tight a control in your own life closes down your options and, in the process, actually limits your choices. As paradoxical as it seems, *Freedom* comes as much from letting go of, as it does from maintaining, control. Your *Freedom* drive will be enhanced by understanding the delicate balance between the two.

MEANING

"The nourishing stew of civilized life doesn't keep bubbling on its own. Put something back in the pot for the people in line behind you," Alan Alda advised his daughter and her classmates at their 1980 college commencement. Our interviewees may not have heard his message, nevertheless they heed his call. Among them are a few outstanding women whose drive is to make the world a better place. For some the quest for meaning is their primary drive. For others it is a secondary motivation. In both cases, meaning is a spark that ignites their fire.

Meaning: a Primary Drive

"Everything in life yearns toward fulfillment. It has got to be beyond money, prestige, self-aggrandizement. If you were to ask me to give my best for a hot dog chain, I might find that difficult. Now, if you ask me to give my best for a Catholic women's college, you've got me."

SISTER MAGDALEN COUGHLIN

Human beings are stubborn seekers of meaning. Rare is the person who does not want to leave the world a better place than she found it. But we know very few people who make it their *raison d'être*. Some of the women we interviewed do. A missionary zeal about their purpose is what gets them up in the morning and it propels and guides them all day.

Felice Schwartz has always been driven by the "possibility to change conditions that I think are intolerable." Her reformist tendencies started early. Fresh out of college after World War II, she attacked the problem of racial discrimination in higher education. This quest arose out of her experience at Smith College, in Massachusetts, where there were only six blacks out of 2,400 students. She decided to do something about that inequity. "I've started from scratch, swimming upstream, twice in my life. Blacks weren't beautiful in 1945." At first, with help from the NAACP and then on her own, this *Twenty-Year-Old Girl* set up the National Scholarship Service and Fund for Negro Students. By getting colleges across the country to open up admission, this organization was responsible for enabling thousands of blacks to get a college education. In the second year of this program, 750 blacks were enrolled in colleges that had never had a black student or only had a few.

Felice next focused her attention on an even larger group facing discrimination, women. She went on to found Catalyst in 1962. This organization works to remove barriers facing women in organizations by tackling issues such as maternity/parental leave, child care, relocation, flexible benefits, and career options for women. Felice has no formal clout with the corporations that need to address these issues. Yet, businesses which protect themselves behind a moat of tradition, are surprised to find themselves letting down the drawbridge for her. Not only do they let her in, they put out the welcome mat. She and Catalyst have helped them find qualified women for their boards of directors, develop child care alternatives for employees, address relocation issues of two-career families, and identify and remove barriers to women's upward mobility. Felice says, "The most rewarding thing in life is to enhance the quality of life for others." She's been doing just that for forty years.

With a different destiny, Ruth Rothstein is also a crusader with a social conscience. She is currently president of Mount Sinai Medical Center in Chicago. This incredible woman has her share of supporters and detractors. Her strength produces results, it also intimidates. Her hospital was originally surrounded by an economically healthy Jewish community. Over the years, the community changed as Jews moved out and less affluent blacks moved in. Ruth took over the leadership of a hospital on the brink of financial disaster. It was in danger of losing its teaching affiliation with a local medical college and a population without the means to pay for medical care was perilously close to losing a hospital. Believing that "everybody needs to get a fair shake," and that everyone, including the poor, deserves to be treated with dignity, she waged a fight to save the hospital.

Not only did Ruth get the hospital on its financial feet in ten years, she set out to rejuvenate the surrounding neighborhood. She spearheaded model projects to revitalize commerce and industry and to develop housing in this previously depressed community.

Ruth's social conscience was born in her Depression era upbringing. She tells a story of her hell fire and brimstone-speaking days as a twelve-year-old on hot summer evenings in Brooklyn. It was a poor neighborhood where people were frequently evicted for their inability to pay the rent. This bobby sox crusader could make Hyde Park out of any street corner. One night when asked by her parents where she was running, she yelled back that she was going to speak at a gathering. They followed hesitantly. Knowing Ruth, they were afraid of what they'd hear. In talking about rent strikes, injustice, and welfare, she admitted to her neighborhood that her family was on relief. Her red-faced father was proud and embarrassed at the same time.

Never afraid to gore someone's ox, this fierce campaigner for justice at twelve went on to be a labor organizer in her twenties. In that role, she accomplished what she considers her most meaningful feat for women. In the late forties and early fifties the United Packinghouse Workers of America had reports of racially discriminatory hiring practices at Swift and Company. They needed proof that black women weren't being hired. Ruth gave the union the proof they needed. She joined a milling throng of women hoping to get hired and watched the crowd disperse when told that Swift was not hiring that day. She showed up at five o'clock the next morning to witness the same scene, only this time Ruth stayed longer. After the black women had left, the whites were taken in by a back door. On the third day, Ruth returned, made eye contact with the hiring boss, and was hired. She had all the proof she needed to help the union win a major grievance. From then on, Swift had to hire black women. Ruth has gone on to win many more battles and *Meaning* still drives her.

It's not hard to have energy when you are doing something you believe in. These women are able to sustain effort over time because what they do is tied to the central purpose of their lives. Making a difference is what they live for.

Meaning: An "Also Ran" Drive

For a larger group of women, *Meaning* is not the dominant thrust of their *Four-Wheel Drive.* However, it is a powerful motivator and their contributions to society's pot are significant. A case in point is Mary Kay Ash, whose secondary drive is her desire to strengthen and empower women.

While Mary Kay is driven by *Challenge,* she also sees the growth and development of women as a meaningful aspect of her business. Her primary goal was never money. "It was to open up an opportunity for women because twenty-two years ago you walked two paces behind the boss and your chances of getting into the executive suite were . . . forget it. I was in the wrong body." To hear her talk about the metamorphosis of women as they grow stronger is to see a proud parent beaming as her fledglings try their wings. She lives to see the transformation of tongue-tied women who at the beginning can't even tell Mary Kay their names. Within six months of loving attention and reinforcement, the evolution from panic to poise is accomplished. The saleswomen gain power and strength while Mary Kay gains meaning and satisfaction. She knows that her company has more women earning over $50,000 a year than any other in the country.

For some of these women *Meaning* is their reason for being; for others it is a secondary drive. No matter. It is a powerful motivator which has implications for you. Your own drive for *Meaning* can lead you to be the best mother or discover the cure for AIDS, or both. If you find yourself procrastinating, or if you feel resistant and lethargic, that may be a sign you are involved in meaningless activity. Nothing will sabotage your drive faster. If, on the other hand, you are engaged in meaningful work, you'll travel full speed ahead. The more connected your activities are to your basic purpose and *Meaning* in life, the more potent the effort and the better your result.

ABOUT DRIVE

The Drive is Excessive

These women are all ambitious strivers. They are not equally driven, but they are all excessively driven. Some *think* they have limited their drive. Ruth Rothstein is one of these. She says she is ". . . perfectly happy to go home and curl up like an embryo and watch television or read. Really, I put in ten and twelve hours a day, five and six days a week. I've earned the right." But many are like Eileen Ford, co-owner of Ford Models, who says that she has a twenty-four-hour job.

Whether they are closer in drive to Eileen or Ruth, excess is the norm of these super-achievers. They are excessive—in their dreams, their achievements, and their effort to realize their goals. As drives go, we think Edy Fee's is pretty extreme. Like Superman, the mild-mannered and traditional demeanor of this AVCO executive and mother of three is deceptive. When she ducks into a phone booth, or in this case the delivery room, she, too emerges with a red "S" on her chest.

The fact that she worked up until the day she delivered each of her three children is not unheard of in this day and age. What is unique is that she spent two hours on the phone immediately after delivering her third child. She was not spreading the good news to family and friends from her bed in the recovery room. She was talking to her office. "I was supposed to lie there for two hours and I had a lot of things on my mind that needed to be taken care of. The child was taken care of and there was a phone, so why not?"

The skeptics among you may be saying, "Yeah, but what does this do to her family?" Edy says, "I have very emotionally healthy children. They'd probably go crazy if I was home." Believe it or not, balance in life is critical to Edy and all her eggs are not in the work basket. But excessive drive is her norm. As with our other interviewees, it is the main propeller on her flight to success.

The Drive is Inevitable

How do these women do it? If you believe Lane Nemeth, it's inevitable. When asked what drives her, this charismatic and energetic president of Discovery Toys said, "I don't know but I do know I have no choice. It's just there and always has been in whatever job I took." This former teacher, who started her own educational toy company in a garage eight years ago, now has generated a 40-million-dollar business.

Gail Koff would agree with Lane. As a partner in Jacoby and Meyers, a mass-appeal, nationwide law firm, she says, "I am driven to make an impact. I have a little voice inside that pushes me forward. It steers me in the right place." With three brothers, all of whom are successful in their fields, Gail stands out as being the most driven. Now she is a parent with two children of her own and notices the same difference in drive between her two kids that her parents must have noticed among their four. Gail is raising them both with the same encouragement and values yet she attributes the differences in drive to their individual makeup. She says, "It [drive] is in the soul of the child."

We think she's right. As though there were an "inevitability syndrome" where drive is concerned, what you see is what you get. It's standard equipment, built in. While we can imagine Gail taking a week's vacation, we can't imagine her permanently altering her pace and striving less. Nor can we imagine Lane Nemeth resting until Discovery Toys has reached the billion-dollar mark that is her goal. (Lane probably won't rest then, either.)

Drive, a cornerstone to success and satisfaction, is activated by a push from the inside, not a pull from the outside. This raises the question, what do you do if you have more dream than drive? You can begin by asking yourself four basic questions geared toward getting you off the dime:

1. Is your dream achievable? Assess whether or not your dream is possible. In this age of technology very little is impossible. Here's the rub. *Things become impossible when we think they are.* Are you squelching your drive with limited thinking?

2. Can *you* achieve this dream? Most things are possible, but experience and skill have to be taken into account. For example, we know it is possible to write computer programs that do almost anything. But the authors of this book have neither the experience nor the expertise (nor the desire) to write any program. (In fact, one of us barely squeaked through a computer literacy course by the skin of her orthodontia'd teeth.) We are still congratulating ourselves and each other for learning to use a word processor.

3. Is the achievement of this dream important and worthwhile to you? For a dream to dredge up drive, it has to touch your core values. What would it contribute to your life? Is it essential to your happiness and well-being? What will be the loss to you if you don't accomplish this dream?

4. Are you willing to pay the price? This big question separates the proverbial women from the girls. Who wouldn't want to be a millionaire? Don't be too hasty in responding. Lee thought she had her answer until she went to a local college class on how to become one. The teacher began the class with the very upbeat statement claiming that everyone in the room could be a millionaire. They would have to do a number of things, though. First on the list of things to do was to drop all non-millionaire friends from your life. Lee didn't wait for item number two. Appalled at the callousness of this statement, she went home. Ten years later she can at least understand the teacher's point. While she hasn't dumped all her non-millionaire friends, she sees clearly the value of surrounding herself with people who represent what she wants to become. She also understands that there is a price to pay for achieving any goal.

YOUR DRIVE WILL REMAIN IN NEUTRAL
UNTIL YOU CAN ANSWER YES TO EACH OF
THESE FOUR QUESTIONS.

Sometimes it's not your own drive that presents the problem. What do you do if you're in overdrive and the people around you—your kids, spouse, colleagues, subordinates—are standing still? You can't shift anyone else's gears. Accepting that limit is a major accomplishment. But what you can do is apply the same four questions to these people so you can understand what drives them. You may even suggest they ask these four questions of themselves. Awareness could be the beginning of change. They may get keys that can help trigger their own motivation and you may come to terms with their level of drive, a level unequal to yours.

The Rewards of Drive

Drive is neither good nor bad, but thinking makes it so. (Excuse the liberal mutation of Shakespeare.) The silver lining of drive glistens seductively and beckons these women to go for it all. In the words of one of our interviewees, "All I want is everything." You have the best chance of getting it when you are driven.

Drive brings rewards. In a society where labeling a woman "ambitious" is still equivalent to Hester Prynne's scarlet letter, these women are refreshingly proud of their success and what it has brought them. Not satisfied with ordinary accomplishments, these 100 driven professionals are unafraid to stick their heads above the crowd. Neither do they apologize—not for their ambition, not for their bank accounts, nor for the other perks that come with success. One of our interviewees lights up when she recalls a situation that occurred at a gas station recently. She pulled in behind the wheel of her sleek Mercedes equipped with its own car phone. The impressed attendant asked if that was her husband's car. Without saying she did it the old-fashioned way, she gave a reply that John Houseman would have been proud of. "No, it's mine. I earned it."

But rewards don't come only in the form of a Mercedes, phone included. These women are rewarded by the intoxication of resisting conformity and being themselves in a world that tries to shape people into conventional molds. These square pegs don't always fit in society's round holes. Instead of whittling off their corners, they carve out square holes. And, in the process they make it all right for other people to do the same.

There are trade-offs, though. Among our interviewees are women who have opted to remain single (15 percent) or childless (30 percent) because of the time and energy relationships would sap from career pursuits. While they recognize the price their career is extracting, it's one they willingly pay. They are rewarded with joy and satisfaction. You, too, can sample the benefits of drive. To help you shift into high gear, take some tips from these excessively driven women:

1. YOU CAN'T SUCCEED WITHOUT DRIVE. Where there is little motivation, there is also little achievement. If you are satisfied with your achievement, your drive is sufficient for your needs. If not, you've got some work to do.

2. REALIZE THAT DRIVE IS AN INSIDE JOB. We aren't all driven by the same things nor to the same degree. Identify which wheels propel your drive and then take action in those areas. If you are not driven by your present work, find out why. Is it boring? Do you find the work meaningless? Has it lost its challenge? Is it constricting? A "yes" answer to any of these questions can shed light on your lack of drive. It also

tells you that you need to make a change, either within your current job or by finding a new one.

3. ABANDON YOURSELF TO YOUR DREAMS. Keep looking for something that will capture your fancy and when you find it, go for it. Stay clear of nay-sayers who tell you that you have lost your balance and moderation. These women show you immoderate drive pays big dividends. Proclaim to the world that you too value excess.

4. USE PAINFUL EXPERIENCES TO INCREASE DRIVE. When the successful women we interviewed were obstructed in one area, they became more driven in another. Look at every situation, especially the seemingly negative ones, as opportunities to develop assets in other areas.

The super-achieving women we interviewed are intemperately and inexorably driven. Without this drive they wouldn't be successful. *Challenge* invigorates, *Change* stimulates, *Freedom* intoxicates, and *Meaning* motivates these potent women. Their relentless drive to accomplish propels them through the rough terrain of life. On this journey, one thing is for certain. They have the energy, the determination, and the motivation to navigate their way successfully. Like the vehicle for which their drive is named, they move steadily and unceasingly through all nature of obstacles on their way to a life of achievement, richness, and fulfillment.

4
MAGNIFICENT OBSESSION

My goal in life is to unite my avocation with my vocation
As my two eyes make one in sight
For only where love and need are one
And work is play for mortal stakes
Is the deed ever really done
For heaven's and for future's sake.

Robert Frost

An intense passion for their work is shared by the 100 women we interviewed. This *Magnificent Obsession* is an infatuation, a real love affair. The objects of their affection are varied. For some, hearts beat faster when they see the latest Dow Jones averages. Others get an accelerated pulse when they're on a construction site breaking ground. Still others get the adrenalin pumping when they see their product's share of the market increase or conditions for the disadvantaged improve. Whether these women are pushing for social change or increased profits, their zeal and their joy are excessive.

Their fervor comes from what syndicated columnist Max Lerner calls the meshing of job and work. Lerner, a

reknowned social commentator in his mid-eighties, still continues to be passionate about his writing and teaching. According to him, a job is what one does for the money necessary to
support oneself. Work, on the other hand, is what one is compelled to do even without financial reward. The ultimate satisfaction is achieved when job and work unite. This unity is the
essence of the love these devout professionals feel for their
work.

Magnificent Obsession brings together *Joy* in the work itself,
a willingness to *Work Hard*, boundless *Energy*, and *Intense
Focus*. The satisfaction and harmony this combination brings
is a reward in and of itself.

Tish Nettleship, CEO of North Pacific Construction Management, a consulting firm that manages major public projects
such as the construction of airports and waste recovery facilities, told us a story that illustrates this reward. Tish recalled
one Saturday when she went to the office at eight in the morning to get caught up on that familiar backlog of work with
which we can all identify. In her beautiful living room-like
office in Santa Monica, the sun was streaming through the
French doors, the logs in the fireplace were burning, and clas-
sical and jazz tapes were playing softly in the background. As
the stack of papers on her desk got shorter, Tish enjoyed one
of those self-contained days when all was right with the world
. . . a transcendant day when she was filled with the inner
peace of creative productivity. Pleased with her accomplishments, she somewhat reluctantly ended her reverie at six that
night. Ten hours had flown smoothly by in total harmony.
After a pleasant dinner with her family she extended the
perfection of a day filled with her favorite things and went to
bed with a stack of business magazines. The first article she
turned to was a quiz boldly titled, "Are You Heading for
Burnout?" Doubting she would qualify, Tish read further.

QUESTION 1: Have you ever gone to the office on a weekend and actually felt you enjoyed being there more that day than you would have enjoyed relaxing with family or friends?
Quiz 1, Tish 0
QUESTION 2: Do you read professional journals at home in bed?
Quiz 2, Tish 0

That's when Tish stopped reading the article. She knew that according to this article, she'd be diagnosed as a basket case heading for burnout. But her experiences told her differently. Recalling the serenity of her rewarding day at the office, Tish knew what she felt and it wasn't burnout. Pleasure, nourishment, and a rejuvenating sense of accomplishment were the bounties of that day.

Going in on a Saturday wasn't a price Tish paid, it was a gift she received. Her way of looking at this voluntary overtime was an eye opener for us. Like most people we know in organizations, we were stuck in the traditional cost/benefit analysis of career commitments. The questions we kept probing revolved around sacrifice and what people have to give up for a job they love. Tish's story and her attitude about work made those questions irrelevant. She found intrinsic pleasure in the experience itself. She wasn't doing it for a payback. There was no price that could be put on the value of what that day gave her.

> "Boredom ages [one] faster than sunshine and worry."
> CONKY JOHNSTON

Magnificent Obsession is more than just a gift, it is also a seductress that inspires following. As we visited these women in their homes and offices, we could feel the energy around them. We noticed the impact their dynamism had on us. We

were inspired over and over again, and we rarely left without
being profoundly affected by their energy and passion for work
they love. It inspired us to expand our own project. An initial
interviewee base of 25 quickly grew to 100. It also motivated
us to do things we hadn't previously considered. Adrienne
Hall showed us the importance of building a power base in the
community. As a result we've started doing just that by becoming board members of the Los Angeles Commission on
Assaults Against Women. Meg Hansson (and so many others)
emphasized how critical it is for women to develop financial
savvy. As a result we now subscribe to three more business
magazines. (We even read them!) Jean Firstenberg moved us
with her commitment to make the American Film Institute a
great library of film as well as the driving force in transforming
film from an exclusively entertainment medium to an art form.
Her passion spoke for itself and, unsolicited, the AFI had two
new members by the time we left her office.

This enthusiasm attracts people like a magnet. Susan Bird,
President of the Committee of Zoo, told us a story that illustrates this effect. There was a famous preacher in England
whose sermons attracted people from miles around. When
asked why people came from far and wide to hear him speak,
he answered, "I'm on fire and they like to see me burn." His
listeners were attracted to the spectacle. More than that, they
were warmed by his fire and they wanted to partake of that
passion.

The women with whom we talked had the same effect on
their "flocks." Much of their power as leaders comes from this
passion and singlemindedness. It creates believers who follow
even in cases where the leadership is exacting and sometimes
less than perfect. We met women who are demanding. They
give 150 percent and expect the same in return. We saw
women who can be curt. They think and move quickly and
expect others to keep pace. We talked with decision makers
who can be mercurial and arbitrary. They frequently give or-

ders rather than seek input. Still, people want to work for them. Why? Because their zeal, which brings with it excessive and sometimes eccentric behavior, is compelling and exhilarating. People who are passionate about their work kindle a fire in others.

Because of this effect, *Magnificent Obsession* is critical for anyone in a leadership role. A manager "on fire" has a better chance of inspiring commitment. CEO's aflame with resolve find it easier to influence boards of directors. Inspired sales people motivate consumers to buy. Even parents, fervent about transmitting values to their children, will have a better chance of effectively doing so if they are intense. People who are zealous in their purpose without proselytizing get followers.

This magnetic draw is important for you to consider if you are in a leadership role—manager, parent, supervisor, teacher —where you are required to influence others. Ask yourself if you are magnificently obsessed. Do you have limitless energy for your job? Do you get up in the morning with eager anticipation about your workday? Do you radiate joy and passion about your work? If you can't even put joy and job in the same sentence, you're about to get some help. In this chapter, you'll see not only what *Magnificent Obsession* looks like, but more importantly, you'll find some ways to bring it into your work.

The all-consuming passion of *Magnificent Obsession* means you'll live life center stage, not in the audience or the wings. This quality, which so enriches the existence of our interviewees and can do the same for you, is made up of four parts: 1. a *Joy* that permeates their lives, 2. a passion that makes them want to *Work Hard*, 3. an endless supply of *Energy*, and 4. a piercing *Focus*.

FUNNY, IT DOESN'T SEEM LIKE WORK

"What do I love about my business? EVERYTHING!"

MARY BAIM

What is most apparent about the obsession of our interviewees is the joy it brings them. They are like kids in a candy store, never able to get enough. It's not that they love every minute of every day because they don't. And it's not that they don't have their share of problems and frustrations, because they do. But their work gives them much more than it takes away and money is often the least of what it gives them.

Judi Missett's candy store was dance even from an early age. Judi is the passionate exercise and fitness devotee whose Jazzercise classes have addicted thousands of women to fitness. She herself is addicted—that's partially what makes her stand out. Being a dancer is not unique. One has only to see *Chorus Line* to know that. Being an exercise leader is not rare. One has only to attend the dime a dozen classes offered in every community to see that. While Judi is talented and good at her job, she is not uncommon in this regard either. But Judi is one of the few people we know who says her *work is play*. Judi radiates as she talks about her passion, Jazzercise. She remembers being excited about dancing since her first dance class at age three. "I always loved to dance. Being a dancer has given me an insatiable amount of energy. Because of that, I get excited about what I do. I'm one of the fortunate few who has been blessed with having a job at which I can make a very nice living while absolutely loving what I do. I get up in the morning thinking, 'Gosh, what do I get to do today? I can be physical, take care of my fitness and be doing a job that gives so much to other people.'" Judi glows with the love of what she does and her passion is shared by the literally hundreds of thousands of women who dance to her tunes.

Judi knows that the roots of her passions may go back to childhood. Sometimes this is true but we don't realize it. If you're fuzzy about your passions, the best way to get in touch with them is to recall your early years. When our interviewees did, their current successes and interests became more understandable. Adrienne Hall, a top advertising executive, showed her skill for good copy early when, as a seven-year-old, she published a neighborhood newspaper. Susan Bird, a real estate developer, showed her entrepreneurial tendencies as a youngster when she set up a business selling popcorn at the free theater in Stephens Point, Wisconsin. She was only eleven years old at the time and transporting 100 bags per trip with the only mode of transportation she had—her doll buggy. Resourceful? Yes. Committed to using their talents? Absolutely. Demonstrating signs early? No question about it.

Do your own backtracking. Begin by remembering how you entertained yourself as a youngster. What were your favorite activities and recurring fantasies? Did they involve working with your hands? Did you seek the opportunity to organize others? Were you good at numbers and puzzles? Did you show a love for words? We would not be surprised if you, like Susan and Adrienne, find the seeds of your calling embedded in your early years. That was certainly the case for Red Burns.

For her, joy comes in the form of "Action, Lights, Camera." Red, the chair of the Interactive Telecommunications Program at New York University met the "love of her life" when she was sixteen. Her date, a graduate student at McGill University, was not that love, but he introduced her to what would be. He captivated her with stories about the National Film Board (NFB) where he was working in 1941 and Red convinced herself that this was the place she had to work. This skinny, freckle-faced kid was too young to get into college, but she did have two tons of perseverence and she'd need every bit of it.

She went to the NFB office everyday for six weeks, parking herself in the hall, determined to get a job. There was a small problem, though. She had no experience, no degree, and no skills. Not surprising then that the man in charge was equally determined not to hire her. He told her not to come back but she ignored his message. Finally, in an attempt to end her six-week siege, this battle-weary man gave her a job and sent her down the hall to a room with desks and typewriters. He thought he was doing them both a favor. But the war was not over. Tenacious Red returned with another demand. This feisty sixteen-year-old girl with nothing to recommend her but her tenacity and intelligence said, "That's not what I want. I want to work here [around film]. I'll do anything, even scrub floors, but I want to work here." The frustrated director, at his wits end, made a deal. He'd give her one more chance to do something, but if that didn't work out, Red agreed to leave. Her obsession won out and her career was born. The six years she spent there were total enchantment. Even though she worked over 100 HOURS A WEEK, she never thought she had a job. Film and media have always compelled her and been the focal point of her professional life. Looking back on her forty-plus-year career, Red says, "I've never thought about the position or the money, only the work. Success is working in a way that allows me to think I don't have a job."

While many people give lip service to loving their work as much as Red does, Betsy Berkhemer-Credaire put her money where her mouth is. This PR entrepreneur loved writing so much she began her career by going to a newspaper and saying, "I'll work for free. Just give me a chance to start here." Betsy's willingness to go-for-broke got her the job and launched her career in journalism. While she didn't work "for free" then, a few years down the road she had to make good on her promise. She had just started her own PR firm and was working out of her apartment. Anyone who has ever started a business can remember the lonely launch that follows the initial jubilation. Betsy was no different. After six months, she got tired of not getting dressed up, not putting on her eyelashes, and not going to work.

Betsy used all her savings to put up first and last month's rent on a small office. Day in and day out, she sat there with her typewriter as her only companion, calling people to drum up business. The first three or four years were rough and there were times she was heavily in debt. Her love of both writing and the interaction with people kept her going. Now, twelve years later, she is president of a top-ranking Los Angeles PR agency, Berkhemer and Kline. She looks for the same hunger that she had as a beginner when she hires people for her company. "I'm most open to people who come to me and say, 'I really want to work here. I've read about your company and I like the clients you've worked for. If you give me a chance, I'll work for free.' " Betsy doesn't expect people to work "for free." However, if you aren't involved in work that you feel compelled to do even without pay, then you're missing out on the joy and passion that work can provide.

> "I'm not on a power track and never have been. I pursue
> the things I want to pursue."
>
> RENA BARTOS

It is clear these female moguls love what they do. But the question we're frequently asked is, "Are they *really* happy and is there room for anything else in their lives? From all indications, they are very happy. There seems to be a low tolerance for the "flatlands" of life. Instead, they experience more peaks and valleys, with the emphasis decidedly on the peaks. They create joy in large and small things and experience it both in and out of work. Because their joy begins with them and permeates whatever they do, they integrate it into their work and their relationships.

As management consultants presenting seminars in companies across the country, we see too few people who radiate joy. Those who show a spark stand out. In a practical sense, their passion makes them more desirable, sought after, and promotable. But more importantly, it adds richness to their lives. In our own work, we can tell when we are magnificently obsessed and when we are not. You probably can, too. It's a lot more fun to feel exhilaration. How much do you love your work? Do you dread getting up in the morning? If so, how frequently —only Monday through Friday? When you are at work, do you watch the clock? Do you play Walter Mitty and dream other people's lives rather than live your own?

Those of us who spend so much time working can ill afford to fritter away life day by day in passionless, joyless ventures. While every day on the job can't be expected to bring a peak experience, it should be giving more than a paycheck and an annual vacation. This is the time to assess what you are getting from your job. Somewhere on the credit side of your ledger should appear the words joy, pleasure, and exhilaration (or their equivalents). Note the balance between the credit and debit sides. Are your scales tipped on the debit side? If so, these women's lives show us that you are cheating yourself out of the richness and joy that work affords. Is that a price you are willing to pay?

If not, start by uncovering your real passions. Make an appointment with a career counselor who has creative ways of getting to your skills and desires. Or conduct your own self-analysis. In addition to recalling what you liked to do as a child, try the following exercise. All that is required is a sheet of paper, a pen or pencil, and an open mind. In the first column, list the skills you enjoy performing and in the next one, the unique competencies you have. Then in the third column, list what you expect from a job. See how your current job stacks up. Does it give you an opportunity to utilize those skills and competencies listed in the first two columns? And does it meet most of the expectations listed in the third? Pay close attention to what your skills and interests are. Investigate possibilities in your areas of interest. Search for the right job as you would for the right mate because It *is* a marriage.

TWENTY-FOUR-HOUR WORKDAYS, BUT WHO'S COUNTING?

"People always want a job like mine. It looks glamorous. It's 10 percent glamour and 90 percent hard work."

ALEXIS ELIOPULOS

The joy these super-achievers find in their work keeps them from being clock watchers. The movie *Nine to Five* was not named for the hours they keep. As hard workers, they focus on getting the job done, not on how long it takes. Because they love their work and their tasks are compelling, they have a high tolerance for long hours and arduous schedules.

It's no accident women with this kind of devotion to the job get to the top. What worked for them can work for you. It did for San Francisco mayor Dianne Feinstein and it did for one of her staff members, who was anything but a nine to fiver. This young clerk at city hall might have remained obscure except for her above-and-beyond-the-call-of-duty kind of dedication. As it happened, the mayor's press secretary, Tom Eastham, came to work on a Saturday to play catch-up. Searching for some information in the basement archives, he heard a noise. The sleuth in him decided to investigate. What he discovered was this clerk covered in dust, buried in files. She'd taken it upon herself to come in on a Saturday to organize some boxes of files for no other reason than it needed doing. When Tom casually mentioned it to the mayor on Monday, she immediately transferred the woman to her office. This previously nameless face now works one room away from the mayor.

It's not surprising that the mayor rewarded this staff member's hard work. She saw in her a kindred spirit. For both, going above and beyond the call of duty is standard procedure. It is hard even to say where the mayor's workday begins or ends because work pervades almost every aspect of her life. It is quite common for her to ride home in her limo giving the city of San Francisco a report card. The notes she makes about litter, potholes, graffiti, and other problems become someone else's top priority the next day. In fact, we wouldn't be surprised if her creative and hard-working staff used their next gift-giving opportunity to put curtains on the windows of her limo. The mayor knows this kind of hard work pays off. Eighty-two percent of San Francisco's voters endorsed her in a recall election initiated by the anti-gun control lobby. That vote of confidence speaks for itself.

What keeps women going at this constant pace? Work that consumes them. It permeates their lives and for many, that's because they grew up in the business. Dorothy Roberts, the cordial and peppy president of Echo Scarfs, was in training for the business as long as she can remember. As a child, her father would take her uptown to the big stores and put her through her paces. He'd tell her to look into a store window, then he'd have her turn around and recite, in copious detail, everything she saw in the window. This was how she learned her keen observation skills that keep her firm in the forefront of the accessory business. Even today, this ardent history buff is teased by those who know and love her best. They say that everything she ever learns ends up on a scarf.

Growing up in her house was a rare and wonderful experience. Scarves were as much a part of family meals as the food. Dorothy's first husband (now deceased) used to joke that the only way he could get away from talking business with her dad was to dive into the pool. Not only did he join her family's business, but Dorothy's children and present husband are part of Echo Scarfs as well. It is a business Dorothy continues to cherish. Maybe that's why she never counts the hours.

"I'm not God. He got the seventh day."

EILEEN FORD

THE IDEA THAT LONG HOURS ARE A REQUIRE-MENT OF SUCCESS IS THE SINGLE MOST CONTRO-VERSIAL ISSUE WE DISCOVERED. At our seminars, it produces the most discussion, resistance, and even anger. People don't want to think that they have to work seventy-plus hours a week to achieve no-holds-barred success. We don't either—when we think only of the hours themselves and what that kind of time takes from other parts of our lives.

But what we also notice is that when we get involved in a project we love, we end up working that many hours (or more) and not balking or even noticing the time. THE NUMBER OF HOURS SPENT TO DO A JOB IS IRRELEVANT WHEN YOU LOVE THE WORK. Putting in the hours is not the issue. "Plugging along" is the antithesis of *Magnificent Obsession.* You can work forty to fifty hours a week, be supremely competent, and love your work. Just don't expect to reach the top of the heap without more effort. We stand on the statement that high level success will remain elusive without working long, hard hours. The question to ask yourself is how hard are you willing to work and will that amount of effort get you the kind of success you desire?

For us, these women gave new definition to the phrase hard work. Our own fifty-hour weeks paled in comparison. Having been schooled in the "work smarter not harder" theory, we got a jolt. Yes, working smart is important, but it is not enough. No one will ever again convince us that working both hard and long isn't an integral part of the success package. We gradually came to the sobering realization that if we weren't willing to put in those long hours, we had better adjust our sights.

SELF-GENERATING DYNAMOS

"I have a lot of enthusiasm whether I'm planting my own garden or working. I'm going to be fifty-six on Saturday and I'm doing seventy-five things."

JUDY ROSENER

That these women have explosive energy is obvious. This dynamic force struck us each time we met another interviewee. Some show it as live-wires who create electrical charges wherever they go. It can be seen in the quickness of their movements, the strength of their voices, the firmness of their handshakes. There is a forceful aura about them. Shrinking violets will not be found among these powerhouses. Another manifestation of energy can be seen in a more understated way. This is the steely strength of quiet power. It registers a gritty determination. While these two energy styles look very different, they are the same in substance. At their root are the physical resources and psychological will to meet life's demands with vitality. Where does this indefatigable energy come from? Some attributed it to the luck of the genes.

Here's what Shirley Hufstedler has to say on the subject. "I picked my ancestors very cleverly. I come from people who had great drive. It's a combination of God-given intellectual gifts and physical endurance . . ." This stamina is what enabled her to survive a grueling schedule in the Department of Education. When President Carter called her to Washington to start that newly created department, she was naïvely excited. Fifteen months later (fourteen-hour days with only Easter, Christmas, and one Sunday off) this woman, no stranger to hard work, was less naïve, and also less excited. In fact, when we asked her if she enjoyed her stint as a cabinet member, she responded with a colorful analogy. She likened the position to swimming across the Amazon River, with two cuts on her legs and the piranhas not far behind. "You don't enjoy the journey but you're very relieved when you make it to the other side." For that tough job, she needed all the energy her genetic luck would provide.

Nobody knows the payoffs of energy better than Judy Rosener, who could have her own thesaurus filled with the numerous titles, epithets, labels, and adjectives that have been used to describe her. Political Tiger. University Administrator. Environmental Activist. Woman of the Year. Limousine Liberal. Grand Jury member. Junior Leaguer. Mother of three. Public television board member. Orange County housewife. Ph.D. (earned in her late forties).

This intelligent, warm, and outspoken woman has a hard time describing herself. It's no wonder. Her evolution over the last twenty-five years from housewife to Assistant Dean of the University of California at Irvine (UCI) Graduate School of Management can be seen in how she addresses herself. The Mrs. Joseph Rosener of the early fifties became Mrs. Judy Rosener in the sixties. Now Dr. Rosener prefers to be called just plain Judy, though she is anything but.

What has changed in her evolution is where she puts her energy but not her vitality, nor her passion for keeping multiple plates spinning. Judy speculates that her energy and joy come from her pluralistic focus. "I think that when you put all your eggs in one basket, you have a problem. I have a family life, a volunteer life, a teaching life, a writing life. The shifting gears helps me not get burned out. My day is so exciting." Judy's joy comes through when she says what very few people could. "If I were to die tomorrow, I've done everything I've wanted to do."

How did this poor youngster from Hollywood manage this feat? In a phrase, energy creates serendipity or what Judy terms "flukes." This gregarious person gets high on making things happen through people connections. The relationships she creates have paid off handsomely. In fact, one that dates back to 1964 resulted twenty years later in saving Judy's job and giving her tenure. Here's how it happened. Knowing that Judy liked to entertain, her cousin suggested that Judy ask the then new UCI vice chancellor over for dinner. Being new to the area, he knew no one. This same man, who later became chancellor, was Judy's ally in her tenure battle to maintain her position as a non-research-oriented professor. She never expected that the relationship born at her "Good Samaritan" dinner in 1964, before she had even considered going back to school, would help her out twenty years later.

Judy's early serendipitous experiences and high energy continued to bear fruit. In 1965, a casual conversation with a professor of organizational behavior led her to become a guinea pig. Dr. Jim March, conducting a study "to see whether thirty-five-year-old middle-aged women could still learn anything," invited her to come back to school. She loved it. She wound up with a master's degree and twelve years later, her Ph.D. We guess Dr. March got his answer.

All her life Judy's energy has been a catalyst. Nowhere is this more obvious than at the university. Here's an example. Arriving early at a Cal Tech Life Member Association get-together, Judy found only Donald Bren, chairman of the Irvine Company, Orange County's dominant and wealthiest development firm. Energetic and gregarious Judy struck up a conversation with Don. When she mentioned where she worked, he told her that he had always wondered why there was no executive development program at UCI. Her response was short and to the point. No money. The next morning his aide called Judy with an offer to underwrite the Executive MBA program to the tune of a $200,000 grant. This was a coup she never intended, another of her "flukes." Her energy and enthusiasm made things happen again.

One of the questions we are most frequently asked about this energy is, "What do you do if you don't have it?" First, curse your ancestors. Then recognize that energy is shown in different ways. Some women's energy is palpable and comes across in vivid bursts. But there is also a quieter energy that looks more like tenacity. These are the proverbial turtles who know how to use their steady pace to win.

Ann Kalman showed us this. This broadcasting executive wanted to move up to Vice President of Promotions at CBS. Though Ann was clearly competent, her boss was not ready to promote her. Instead of wasting her energy being upset, Ann designed a two-year campaign that involved enhancing her boss's image as well as her own. By the time he promoted her, it was such a popular decision that it made them both look good. Ann showed durable energy in sustaining a long and patience-sapping process. What's more, she'll continue her perseverance because Ann observes that in the old-boy network of the broadcasting world, she still has to work twice as hard as a man to get ahead.

Energy, whether the burst or tenacity version, is clearly necessary. If you still think you need more, then it is time to look at exercise as an energy generator. It is a prime strategy for recharging your battery.

Let's Get Physical

> "When a person is athletic and can do something with the body, you walk a little taller, your strides are a little peppier, your movements are a little more secure, and you feel good about yourself.
>
> JUDGE JOAN DEMPSEY KLEIN

It is no coincidence that the highest energy women we talked with were those involved in physical activity. If someone went to an energy doctor to remedy sagging vitality, the number-one Rx would be Olivia Newton John's message, "Let's get physical."

In a group of highly energetic women, Sheila Cluff and Judi Missett stand out. As fitness gurus who live the message they teach to others, they are emphatic in attributing the accomplishment of their goals to the high energy they get from exercise. But they are not the only ones.

Roberta Weintraub would give them a run for their money. This Los Angeles School Board member and television talk show host maintains a rigorous exercise regimen. She rises daily at 4 A.M. to read two newspapers and then begins exercising at 6. She never misses a day. Roberta walks five miles each day with weights, works out fifteen to thirty minutes in her home gym, and one day a week, she has a trainer come to her home for a one and a half hour workout. At age fifty-one, Roberta lifts weights and bench presses her own weight. She has been through some trying times, the most painful of which was the loss of her son in an automobile accident. Further, heading the Board of Education of a sprawling, angry metropolitan school district during the stresses of integration was certainly no picnic. Exercise is one of the things that saved her. She says, "It's extremely important to exercise in order to keep your mental well-being. I've been through some tough things in my life and exercise has made a lot of difference—not all the difference, but a lot."

Many of our other interviewees also know that exercise begets energy. They include physical activity in their schedules as a way to prime their energy pumps. Jane Hurd balances out her flute playing with aerobics. Henrietta Holsman sails competitively (and for fun, too) with her Wellesley Alums. Red Burns and Frankie Cadwell swim in the mornings before work. Tish Nettleship relishes river rafting and skiing with her six children. Maryles Casto and Ann Kalman put their husbands through their paces when they run with them in the morning.

Jane Evans and Muriel Siebert make time to play tennis twice a week. And on and on and on . . .

There is no better return on investment than physical exercise. Do you have enough energy to do all the things you want to do in your life? If not, take a step in the right direction—brisk walking will do for starters. You can organize a lunch walk group at work. An after hours aerobics class will revitalize an end of the day sagging energy. If you'd rather bounce and jump in the privacy of your own home, investigate the numerous exercise video tapes and equipment and get the one that suits your style. Whatever you do, get moving.

Making Things Happen

If exercise is the first prescription for sagging energy, then accomplishment is the second. Electrically charged Judi Missett says, "If I'm not productive, then I don't have any energy. The more I accomplish, the more energy I have to do even more. When I'm depressed, it's usually because I'm not getting things done." Her aerobic counterpart Sheila Cluff dances to the same tune when she says, "I get a joy or thrill out of doing things well. Accomplishing things spurs me on to accomplish more." Making things happen energizes them both.

No one can be high energy and active all the time. Even these dynamos, with all their vitality and accomplishments, get down and out. We could not imagine them getting the ordinary "blahs" but we also know they are human, so we asked Sheila Cluff how she combats her low energy cycles. Her method for dealing with low energy was sane and fairly simple. When the blahs take over, she knows she has lost her focus. Her strategy is to go back to basics. Reorganize. Take stock. Categorize. It might be only her closets and drawers she attacks, not her whole business empire, but it works. It snaps her out of the doldrums and gets her moving again. The message for you? When you can't get moving, find any corner of your life you can organize and control. Start small. Get mastery of small areas and that energy and momentum will build. Here are some other bits of wisdom that we have consolidated from 100 different women.

Get Going and Keep Going Tips:

1. *Inspire Yourself.* Surround yourself with people who are nurturing and stimulating. Get rid of toxic or negative elements in your life. Expose yourself to ideas and information that are challenging and provocative. Meet with friends, mentors, and experts in certain fields. *Read, read, read.* Take a class at a local university or community college. Try your library, bookstore, or newspaper for inspiration. In some way, fill your initiative cup full of stimulating, vibrant people and ideas, and your own energy will truly runneth over.

2. *Pace Yourself.* Remember that every journey of a thousand miles begins with a single step. Search out a beginning point, no matter how small the step. Make that call. Get the information or set up an appointment. You will help yourself by balancing long and short range goals, and by breaking them down into smaller pieces.

3. *Entice Yourself.* Give yourself a treat. Begin with a part of the task you like to do and will enjoy. As you survey the "meal of life," this might be a time to eat dessert first.

4. *Commit Yourself.* Act wholeheartedly and commit to both yourself and to others. Make a pact with someone else that will ensure your taking action. Broadcast your plans and goals to friends who will keep you honest and hold you accountable.

5. *Confront Yourself.* Acknowledge when you fall short on your commitments. Pay attention to your own resistance when you see yourself balking and procrastinating. Ask yourself why and listen to your responses. Are you pursuing actions because they are *your* priorities? The resistance may be a signal that you are attempting to implement someone else's "shoulds." It may be a clue that you are in over your head and need more money, more time, more training, or more resources of various kinds. The information you get can signal future action.

6. *Nudge Yourself.* Set goals and expectations for yourself that are challenging but realistic. Maintaining the balance between high expectations and achievable ends is critical. You won't have energy for aims that seem unreachable. Set them 10 to 15 percent beyond your comfort level so you can gently nudge your own growth. The challenge can exhilarate you.

7. *Celebrate Yourself.* Build in rewards and "can hardly waits." Enjoy the doing, not just the accomplishment. Reward yourself with time or with your own special treat. Use celebration as a rejuvenator. It will increase your energy and continue to make things happen.

LASER-LIKE FOCUS

While these women balance many plates with verve, don't get the idea they are fragmented. They are capable of honed focus and powerful determination. Their concentration is la-

74 WHAT IT TAKES

ser-like, blocking out any distractions that could divert them from their goals.

The ability to wear blinders temporarily keeps Jane Hurd, CEO of Children's Hospital in Los Angeles, on target. "I'm not married and I don't have children. I've been able to single-mindedly devote the time and energy to my career." However, all work and no play would make Jane a dull girl and she has no intention of allowing that. "When I play, I really play. I have friends, hobbies, play the flute, work jigsaw puzzles, travel, and dance. When I'm at Children's Hospital, I'm here and focused. When I'm not, I'm able to walk away from the job." Like Jane, some of the women we talked with are able to leave work at the office. Others can never leave it behind. But they all have this ability to concentrate and block out distractions.

To do that, they are clear about their priorities and have learned not to deviate from the path to their objectives. They don't stay on this path by saying "yes" to all the myriad requests and interruptions that come their way. Their willingness to say "no" and risk the disapproval and rejection that are a frequent response is another quality that sets them apart.

One of the most focused women we interviewed is Marilyn Barnewall, a premier consultant to America's largest banks. She may hang her hat in Aurora, Colorado, but she travels a good deal of the time. Being in the presence of this financial whiz is the equivalent of being caught up in the vortex of a cyclone. Because intense concentration is as much a part of her as breathing, Marilyn used to take it for granted, but not any more. As Marilyn tells the story, "I didn't know I was different until I worked at United Bank of Denver and some guy said, 'Boy that person is almost as intense as you are Barnewall!' And I said, 'You think I'm intense?' That's when I started appreciating my energy." Our response to Marilyn's question about her intensity would have been, "Does a leopard have spots?" Her laser-like focus and intensity combine to make her the sought-after consultant she is.

She demonstrated this focus with one of her clients when she went to do a one-day seminar for a South Carolina bank. "This group of guys wasn't giving me the kind of respect I'm used to getting. It was costing them $2,500 to $3,000 to have me there. The vice president of the board walked in late with a kind of I'm-not-settled-I'm-not-ready-to-hear-what-you-have-to-say attitude. I said to the group, 'Tell you what, it seems to me you're a little unsettled this morning so what I'm going to do is what all the public speakers say you should do. I'm going to tell you a joke and I want you to *LAUGH REAL HARD*. Then I'd like you to settle down so I can do what you're paying me a lot of money to come down here and do today.' That got the room quiet." Marilyn's intense focus continually makes her a person to be reckoned with. Wherever she works, she brings her I-mean-business attitude.

People who have trouble sustaining Marilyn's kind of intensity can take a lesson from Edy Fee, vice president of Avco Financial Services. You remember her as the person who called the office from the recovery room after delivering her third child. Wanting to improve her already superb time management skills, Edy went to a time management workshop and heard what many of us have heard before, "Do one thing at a time." The difference is she took it to heart and made it a keystone of her success strategy.

Edy had an ingenious way to put this advice into practice. Most people can identify with the knee-jerk reaction of turning on the radio or putting in a tape as soon as you get in the car. That's not what Edy does anymore. While she drives, she concentrates not on motivational tapes or the radio, but on the road ahead. Training herself to do only one thing at a time is how she honed her concentration skills. "Focus, not spray" could now be her motto. It enables her to manage a complex life—husband, three children, community activities, and a demanding job that requires travel. Her focusing works. In terms of time, this practical technique gives Edy the biggest bang for her buck.

If you'd like to hone your own concentration skills, you can begin by analyzing where you fritter away moments. Do you find your attention splintered among many projects and goals? If you frequently find yourself physically in one location and mentally in another (or several others) you are minimizing your effectiveness. At times like this, bring yourself back to the task at hand. Play mental games by setting time limits and rewarding yourself. When your mind wanders, capture your thoughts quickly on paper. Keep pads of paper and pencils in purses, in cars and by bedsides. Knowing that you won't forget these ideas will keep you from being distracted. This narrowing of focus may not come easy because we live in a society that laughs at people who "can't chew gum and walk at the same time." But try it. We believe doing one thing at a time will get you on the right track and keep you there.

HAS THE TEETER TOTTERED?

Sure these women are successful, but what is the effect of this *Magnificent Obsession* on the rest of their lives? Can they possibly have other parts to their existence or will the only warmth they get on a cold night come from their success? Our own observation after dealing with this same issue 100 times over is that the balanced life is probably more myth than reality and very individually defined. What is it and by whose standards? The answer to the frequently asked question, "Can these women who are so passionate about work live lives with balance?" is both yes and no.

YES, their lives are balanced in that they are rich, full, exciting, and they encompass loving, supportive relationships. But they run the full emotional gamut. They can also be exhausting, exasperating, and full of stress. NO, in that their lives are not divided so that every facet gets equal time. Most tilt their time commitments toward work. Some call themselves workaholics, some vehemently reject that label. We couldn't see any difference between the two. They perform the same juggling act other professional people do and deal with the same pulls, tugs, and regrets that conflicting priorities create. But they are more exhilarated by their lives' diversity than frustrated by it. As a group they are also happier and more satisfied than most anyone we know. They like their lives and relish the various places they put their time and energy as they busily juggle personal and professional agendas.

Sure, these dynamos sometimes feel guilty about the time their demanding careers take from their kids. And, on weekends, when they are home spending time with family, they feel the tugs of briefcases that remain unopened. It's not that our interviewees never experience the same conflicting priorities that other women feel. But they are freer from these conflicts because their passion gives them greater clarity and focus. The result is that they give themselves 100 percent to whatever they're doing, and most of the time, this means doing the work they love. That is a price they gladly pay for the gift of joy they receive in return. Even so, the tugs are ever present.

No one's tug story tops Barbara Casey's. Barbara, now owner of her own PR firm, Casey and Sayre in Malibu, found out the hard way that family and work demands sometimes clash. She had her first child in 1971 when she was vice president in charge of PR at Kaufman and Broad. Barbara was in labor, ready to go to the hospital, when she got an emergency phone call from the office. Her boss, Eli Broad, had been involved in a helicopter crash in Israel. Though he survived, the situation was fraught with tension because of the impact the crash might have had on the company's stock. Barbara was needed to write a quick press release to allay fears and maintain stability. When she told the secretary that she literally had a more pressing engagement in the delivery room, the irritated secretary responded, "Couldn't you just stop over on the way?" After meeting this effervescent woman, we have no doubt that she can handle many things, but this is a little too much to expect, even of her.

Dr. Nannerl Keohane, president of Wellesley College, feels the tugs, too, as she juggles a college presidency with a marriage and four children. She recalls a painful incident when she was forced to miss her son's school award dinner because it was scheduled the same night as a cocktail party and dinner in her honor, planned eighteen months previously. Her guilt and sense of loss at missing some meaningful moments are mitigated at those times when she sees the benefits her children gain from her career.

She tells a story in *Independent School* magazine about her son, Nathaniel, who was then eleven years old. At that age he was still ambivalent about both girls and his future career, although he could boil down his career choices to either a biologist or an astronomer. His solution to the career dilemma was that he would be the astronomer and he'd marry a biologist. Of this incident, Nannerl says, "Somehow, that moment went a long way toward making everything worthwhile—the busyness [sic], the guilt that accompanies a two-career marriage of two hard-working parents, the unbaked cookies—all that, for the moment, disappeared. Nathaniel had seen through the problems to the heart of the matter: that building a strong relationship on two careers means multiplying your own enjoyment and access to the world. Instead of trying to excuse, explain, legitimate the two-career family, he saw it as a wonderful new handle on the world." For that moment, the tugs disappeared, but balance is still an issue that is intimately tied to the core of *Magnificent Obsession*.

If there were an "equal time ammendment," Adrienne Hall would be its author. Balance is her battle cry. A recent L.A. *Times* article quoted her comments at a panel for UCLA

Graduate School of Management students. "I can't think of a better way to define balance than to say it is the art of having more than one basket to put our eggs into and then having the talent and the zest and the drive to gather as many eggs as possible.

"Lead a balanced life. By its very nature, balance implies being able to keep your toes on the tightrope, to make it across the years with enough resilience to swing a little, love a little, laugh a little. And it means that—even hanging by a thread— you'll never fall off."

Any person able to keep up with Adrienne's hectic pace would see she is that skillful tightrope walker. When we interviewed her at her home on a Saturday morning, she rushed in from a nine o'clock meeting, fresh warm croissants in hand. As we talked with her, we learned she stays on the tightrope but it's never been easy. Her kids are now grown but they weren't in 1960 when she and Jane Levine opened what Adrienne believes was the first advertising agency in the country owned by women. It was a demanding juggling act, but she managed it. She gives credit to the fact that she's had the same housekeeper for twenty-five years, a husband with a flexible professional life, and two sets of grandparents nearby. It is not surprising that balance is a high priority for Adrienne. She knew from the time she was a child that she wanted to get married, have four children, and work. She has done all of that.

Adrienne is sensitive to the difficulties of balancing career and family. Having been both an entrepreneur and a corporate executive, she says that maintaining the balance is easier in the entrepreneurial arena. Her suggestion to those of you who want to stay in the corporate environment is to be creative in how you plan your life. Seek out companies that are more progressive in day care and that have more liberal policies toward maternity leave.

Long hours and hard work—*loved* and *enjoyed*—are the es-

sence of *Magnificent Obsession.* The boundaries between work
and personal life are not discreet. A consuming passion by its
very nature can't be limited to an eight-hour day.

Work doesn't end when these women leave the office. After
hours, work goes home with them, to parties and other busi-
ness/social engagements. Work has even been known to take
up major suitcase space on vacations. Marilyn Lewis, as the
creative chairman of the board of Hamburger Hamlet Restaurants, finds the lines blurred between home and work. "My
private life and my professional life are one. I don't know the
difference from one to the other." In fact, Marilyn and her
husband can't go out to eat in a restaurant now without counting seats. When she looks into a dining room, she sees not
customers but "turn-over rate, labor costs per hour, and equipment cost." They have just remodeled the kitchen in their
home so it can serve as a test kitchen for new restaurant reci-
pes. For the Lewises, work is life. They've hardly taken a vacation in over twenty years but you won't catch them complaining. They love what they do.

Working twenty-four hours a day can take its toll on family
life. Perhaps Marilyn, as well as some others with whom we
talked, have found a way to minimize that toll by working
with spouses and/or children. In so doing, guilt at not being
more available to husbands and kids may be lessened, and
being in the trenches together can strengthen family bonds.
However, working with family can also have its drawbacks.
Relaxing dinner conversations may end up becoming narrowly
focused and occasionally quarrelsome work discussions.

In some cases, spouses who work together had difficult periods negotiating a satisfactory balance of power. For a while,
they experienced increased tension both at home and at work.
Irene Cohen, for example, found it difficult to share the deci-
sion-making power with her husband, who is her chief financial officer. She liked calling the shots and didn't relish sharing
the control of what started out as her business. She and her

husband, Sy, have found a way to delineate responsibilities at work and leave their egos at home. All is well for them now but overlapping professional and family lives can be a double-edged sword. While these successful women who mix work and home together admit there are pros and cons to the overlap, they genuinely like the choices they have made.

At the heart of *Magnificent Obsession* is the passion, joy, and commitment these women feel toward their work. For all of us who work, the questions are simple to ask, but sometimes hard to answer. Do you feel this kind of joy and passion about your work? If not, is it because you've never seen work in that light—as a potential source of deep satisfaction and fulfillment? Are you a person who values and understands all that *Magnificent Obsession* is, but won't ever experience it as long as you remain in your present job? If so, what are you willing to do about it? These are tough questions and the lives you've glimpsed hand you the full-length mirror. This is truth-telling time. There are no "right" answers, only questions that help you find your own way to infuse your life with joy, passion, and energy. If you'd like to get the ball rolling but don't know how, here are a few suggestions.

1. *Have a strongly developed work ethic.* Like it or not, getting ahead and hard work go hand in hand. Recognize that putting limits on your work hours also puts limits on your success.

2. *Work at what you love.* Make it a point to find a job where you don't think about watching the clock. It is easier to tolerate long hours when your work is a consuming passion. You'll also get a bonus when you find that your efforts bring you not only a paycheck but joy and satisfaction as well.

3. *Limit the number of objectives you pursue at any one time.* Trying to do it all at once usually results in achieving nothing. Eliminate distractions and concentrate on the present moment. Reward yourself for narrowing your focus and for not doing ten things at once. Focus your energy—it will increase your results.

4. *Give energetic commitment to whatever you do.* Abandoning yourself wholeheartedly to your pursuits is your best chance to achieve joy and vitality. Take pride in your excessiveness.

Our own observation after witnessing 100 paragons of success is that having a *Magnificent Obsession* is a blessing and a gift. It gives far more than it takes. It is what enables these women to work long, hard hours while maintaining energy and concentration. Work is one of their primary loves and an enormous part of their lives. It exhilarates them, brings them energy, and gives them joy. It is their *Magnificent Obsession* and they make no apologies for it.

5
MEGAVISION

"I have the potential of Eleanor Roosevelt and Golda Meir.
My fear is that I won't live up to it."

BARBARA BALSER

LaRae Orullian, president of Women's Bank of North America, wants to change the power in the upper echelons of banking, an industry where 65 percent of the work force is female, but only 2 percent of the managerial positions are held by women.

Bettye Martin Musham, president and CEO of Gear, Inc., was the originator of concept selling in home decorating. She was the first to coordinate all home decorating needs from wallpaper and paint to towels, linens, and curtains in one place.

Jean Firstenberg, Director of the American Film Institute, is creating the "Smithsonian of Celluloid." Her dream is to show the history of film and have film be regarded as an art form, not just an entertainment medium.

How many people do you know who have this high level of aspiration? We talked with many women who do. They want to leave their mark in a big way. Making an impact to them does not mean making a few ripples in a pond. Tidal waves are more their style. Neither they, nor their accomplishments, can be ignored. They shoot for monumental goals. As sculptors, they wouldn't produce birdbaths. You're talking Mount Rushmore. As field generals, they'd be strategizing the Battle of Gettysburg, not occupying themselves with roadside skirmishes. As women who see the world in epic proportions, they find exponential possibilities in each undertaking. You will not catch them being nay-sayers, shutting down their options. Their passion for saying "yes" to life is rooted in their Gibraltaresque faith in themselves. That rock-solid belief gives them the confidence to make their dreams a reality. As implementers of the audacious, they have the daring of David attacking Goliath. The combination of *Grand Scale-Thinking, 360-Degree Vision,* and *Chutzpah* coalesce to form *Megavision* in action.

Why is *Megavision* important? What can it do for you? For starters, it removes limits to your success. Without it, you'll be prevented from being the most effective parent, stimulating teacher, convincing lawyer, motivating manager, or successful entrepreneur. It is the quality that causes you to aim for greatness. It is also the quality that stirs your discontent with what is, to strive for something better. A dose of *Megavision* is at the root of all but accidental progress. It eliminates boredom, and means continual growth and achievement. With *Megavision,* the possibilities are tantalizing.

But *Megavision* has a down-side, too. Those who have it live in what one of our colleagues calls a state of "divine dissatisfaction." Seeing new possibilities at every turn makes it difficult for these megavisionaries to be satisfied with the status quo. They rarely give themselves the luxury of relaxing their expectations or resting on their laurels. This doesn't mean that these women are frantic and unable to enjoy their accomplishments. But their minds are always ten steps ahead, thinking of their next three projects. To some people, this sounds exhausting. To them, it's exhilarating. For still more on the down-side —they do run the risk of being rejected because of the audacious size of their dreams. People who don't have their vision or courage may express disapproval or scorn, but like Rhett Butler, frankly, they don't "give a damn." The voice they listen to comes from inside.

Megavision is a rare and intriguing quality. This kind of thinking is not common among the people we know, do business with, or teach. In a world where the knee-jerk response is frequently "No," these possibility thinkers are like salmon swimming upstream. For some of the interviewees, seeing possibilities is instinctive. It's a quality they've had from childhood. But those of us who aren't natural megaseers can take heart. Many of these women developed this quality experience by experience. The purpose of this chapter is to show you how to develop it, too. Whether an individual is born with *Megavision* or builds it step by step, the result is the same—a way of looking at the world that combines *Grand-Scale Thinking, 360-Degree Vision,* and *Chutzpah.*

GRAND-SCALE THINKING: THE CANYON, THE TETONS, AND THEIR DREAMS

"Set your goal at least one peg higher than you think [possible] and be doubly prepared at each rung."

GAIL WINSLOW

Bigger is not always better; it is only bigger. But if one wants to leave a mark and influence the course of events, then bold action on a grand scale is required. In any arena, the bigger the goal, the greater the potential impact. One environment we can all identify with is school. A classroom teacher with high aspirations for self and students can change the lives of those who go through her doors. In a bigger arena, a school principal who demands the best from her teachers can win the battle for effective education in her school, and even impact an entire community. Dr. Maria Montessori, founder of the Montessori method of education, had still a larger scope. Her theories and techniques transformed not only the educational system of Italy but that of the Western world. While her work is not necessarily more significant than that of an excellent teacher or a superb principal, it has wider influence. This monumental scope is the essence of *Grand-Scale Thinking*.

Big scale has not traditionally been viewed as an attractive quality in women. Neither has boldness. In appearance, small and petite have been the feminine ideals. In manner, demure and deferential have been considered appropriate. Can you even imagine a female counterpart for Paul Bunyan or the Incredible Hulk? Subliminally, the message that big and bold are not beautiful for women has carried over. Women have not historically gotten their M&M's for bold plans and big dreams. The women we talked to have defied tradition and risked disapproval to think and act on a grand scale. By shedding the limits of their own and others' thinking to accomplish all their potential would allow, they have demonstrated that big can be beautiful, but achieving it hasn't been easy.

Just ask Muriel Siebert, Linda Alvarado, and Marilyn Barnewall. The fact that a woman had never held a seat on the New York Stock Exchange didn't mean Muriel Siebert shouldn't have one. Having no background in the male-dominated world of construction did not stop Linda Alvarado from building one of Denver's most successful construction firms. Not having a Harvard or Stanford MBA behind her did not keep Marilyn Barnewall from presenting her own antidote for a troubled national economy before one of Paul Volcker's committees. Muriel, Linda, and Marilyn have big dreams and the *Chutzpah* to match. Like them, the visionaries whose stories we tell are rewriting what are acceptable, desirable accomplishments for women and continually adding new chapters.

One of the most far-reaching visions belongs to Kathy Keeton, president of OMNI Magazine. Kathy's big ideas started when she was a youngster. As a South African farmer's daughter recovering from polio, she was preoccupied with science fiction. That preoccupation has turned into a career bringing science to lay readers. Kathy's science bent coupled with her *Grand-Scale Thinking* can best be seen in this quote from her futuristic book *Woman of Tomorrow.*

> Women in all walks of life need to move beyond technopeasantry. But more than that, women need to carve out careers in scientific and technological fields. It's not enough for women to want to be lawyers, executives, and politicians. The future is shaped by those who generate new knowledge, create new products, and find new options for solving the problems of humanity —hunger, overpopulation, energy and other resource shortages . . .

Kathy envisions a future vastly different from what we are living, one that delineates such radical social changes as communities in space and robots in the home. She sees that the future lies in science and technology, fields where women are traditionally underrepresented. Her leitmotif is to have women put themselves at the front of the scientific/technological parade, not bring up the rear where they usually march. She would like to see a world where women harness science and technology, the most powerful forces today, for change in the world, rather than become victims of these forces.

But Kathy's big ideas don't stop at the conceptual level. Her magazine and her book help women integrate technology into their lives. While the new concepts in birthing technologies, lengthening life span, and restructuring communities are not

her creations, taking these ideas from the sterile environment
of the scientific laboratory into the living rooms of America is
her gift. Her book translates abstract concepts into practical
application. She shows women concrete, meaningful ways to
involve technology in their lives. For example, Kathy tells
women:

> . . . to be informed enough to be active in matters that affect
> our future. You may not mastermind a communications satellite
> that brings educational programming to remote villages of the
> world, but you may have to help decide whether the PTA
> should spend its money on science lab equipment or on a new
> football stadium. You can certainly tell your representatives
> what you think of the lack of funds for research on test-tube
> fertilization when the local utility company is deciding whether
> to invest in solar technologies or strip mining. You bring video
> recorders, "smart" telephones, digital TVs, and computers into
> your home, and you have the power to use them in ways that
> strengthen your family and contribute to a fair division of labor
> around the house.

Kathy's big picture vision has implications for women everywhere. While few of us are involved in advocating such
dramatic changes as Kathy does, we can all think bigger than
we do. We can be receptive to the technology she advocates
and stop telling ourselves and our daughters that we don't
have a mind for math and science.

Meg Hansson, who has a mind for both, shows us big vision
from the entrepreneur's point of view. Before we tell you about
her vision, we want to tell you a little bit about Meg. If you
look in the Boulder, Colorado, phone book, you'll find her
listed as "product developer." While accurate, the title is limiting and does not begin to do her justice. Meg, by profession, is
an entrepreneur but she calls herself a "shameless
brainpicker." Her mind is like a high powered computer, stor-

ing information, connecting ideas, and spitting out schemes at the blink of an eye. How does she manage this? Meg stores what she learns because she has a belief that everything connects, that sooner or later it will become useful.

Meg's present big idea does no less than tackle monumental global problems like famine and water pollution. Addressing these problems is more than dinner conversation for her. She puts energy behind her *Grand-Scale Vision* in several ways. At the time of the interview, her number-one business project was PureCycle, Inc., which aims to give people pure water by attacking such problems as contamination of water supplies, sewage disposal, and maintaining water levels. She continues to put her energy behind projects that have a worldwide impact. She serves on the boards of several banks to help bankers see the world with a more global perspective. She brings lateral, creative thinking to a conservative industry's linear and logical method of tackling problems. While she recognizes that banks are in business to make money, she brings the perspective that the world's well-being is tied up with more than the bottom line. Rather than limiting their vision on the issue of debtor nations to the fiscal arena, she urges bankers to look at education and social systems as avenues rich with potential for solving what on the surface are economic dilemmas.

Meg wasn't born wanting to tackle world hunger but she always did think big. Like any eight-year-old, Meg was going to make her fortune in lemonade. However, in a Henry Ford way, she got a better idea when they closed a local street to traffic and opened it to skating after school. Even at a young age, she saw a ripe opportunity and she seized it. Meg borrowed money from her mother, filled garbage cans with ice, and sold cans of soda pop. She got her earliest lessons in profit margins when she found it cost much more to buy soda wholesale than to make lemonade from the free ingredients in her mom's kitchen. By the time she repaid her mother and her own savings account, there was little profit. But she parlayed this learning into a very profitable venture two years later.

As a wizened entrepreneur of ten, she stumbled onto an ad for plum pudding. Never one to miss an opportunity, she ordered it and resold it for Christmas gifts. She made between $300 and $400 (the equivalent of several thousand dollars today) and her profit earned 3 percent interest. She did this for four years and says that her profit margin in that venture was among the best she's ever had. When she went away to school at fourteen, people were still calling her wanting to order their pudding.

The same grand scale instincts that got her involved in soda and plum pudding as a youngster told her that baby boomers would create their own baby boom. When she combined that information with the increasing emphasis on fitness and outdoor activity, she cut her adult entrepreneurial teeth on Jericho backpacks for babies. The same antennae led her to obtain the sole distribution rights for umbrella strollers, a success story that matches Jericho backpacks. She continues to get in and out of projects. In so doing, she sees both success and failure. Neither throws her. Some of her six-thousand-dollar investments have returned a quarter of a million dollars. Other projects have gone defunct. Meg has no fear of failure, only a fear of not thinking big enough.

As you read about Kathy and Meg, you may wonder if there is hope for anyone who didn't have big dreams at seven. Helen Galland gives us that hope. She learned her *Grand-Scale Thinking* step by step and experience by experience.

We imagine there are many of you who, like Helen, got your work baptism in the world of retail. If you're like us, you undoubtedly didn't even know what CEO stood for back then. Helen probably didn't either. Starting out as a young sales trainee at Lord & Taylor in 1945, she never dreamed that thirty-five years later she would become president and CEO of Bonwit Teller. As a novice, her sights weren't set on running a thirteen-store, $100 million retail chain. Instead Helen focused on doing a superb job at every step along the way. As she proceeded up the ladder—buyer, manager, vice president, CEO—her sights increased. So did her impact. Now *Grand-Scale Thinking* has become second nature to her. She has leveraged her training and experience into a business of her own. As president of Helen Galland Associates, a marketing and business counseling service with retail clients at home and abroad, she now teaches other people to think on a grand scale.

You don't have to be CEO of a department store chain as Helen was or tackle the problem of technological literacy as Kathy does to have *Grand-Scale Thinking*. You can think big at home, in the office, in the classroom, or in the boardroom. *The key is to keep enlarging your sights.* Our suggestion to you is to put yourself in arenas that are larger than your comfort zone. If you're used to making presentations in front of your department, make one for the whole company. If you've only thought of a promotion one level up, set your sights higher. Look toward top levels of management, or even to starting your own company. If you're working on a fund raiser, don't be limited by last year's earnings. Wherever you choose to put your energy, think bigger.

Another way to broaden your horizons is to use visualization techniques. Try the following. Take some quiet time to dream and fantasize about your ideal life. In fact you might even pretend you're Steven Spielberg and let the child in you come out as you focus on your inner movie screen. Design your life to be everything you want. See yourself enjoying the fruits of your achievement. Note the details in your surroundings. See colors—specific, real, and clear. Pay attention to your environment. Be very conscious of sights, sounds, and smells. Imagining these pictures to be your reality is the first step in making it so. Repeating this process frequently increases your chances of making them come to life. Think of your dreams regularly before you go to sleep at night, when you're exercising in the morning, or whenever you have a quiet moment. Don't nay-say them. These fantasies are the sources of your *Grand-Scale Thinking*.

360-DEGREE VISION

"Learn to recognize opportunity without being opportunistic."

DIANNE FEINSTEIN

"Life is a room with an open door."

IRENE COHEN

The quality that goes hand in hand with *Grand-Scale Thinking* is *360-Degree Vision,* a perception which allows you to see possibilities everywhere. It keeps your mind open to alternatives by finding connections in the most unlikely places, and by viewing the world in a non-conventional way.

Among those with *360-Degree Vision,* Sheila Cluff, owner of two health spas in Ojai and Palm Springs, stands out as an unparalleled possibility seer. She spews out new ideas like an air popper pops corn. We didn't need this perception reaffirmed but it was, the day we ate lunch with her at a conference for women in business. "Hello, I'm-so-and-so-what's-your-name-and-what-do-you-do?" Anyone who has ever been to a professional networking function recognizes this perfunctory greeting.

However, in Sheila's case, an ordinary social amenity is transformed to produce extraordinary results. Here's what happened. Sitting at our round table of eight was a young woman who publishes a local paper in Alpine, a small town near San Diego. In less than three minutes, Sheila saw the possibilities for a mutually beneficial connection and grabbed it. She warmly introduced herself to the quiet and unassuming conference attendee who might have passed unnoticed at someone else's table. Upon hearing what this publisher did, Sheila immediately told her about the health/fitness column she writes, which is generally sold to newspapers and other publications. In the case of smaller papers, though, she often makes trades. She offered to trade her column for advertising space. In less than three minutes, they made a deal.

What we saw at that conference was just a snapshot of what goes on in Sheila's life all the time. She is proud of her un-canny ability to see the way things connect. She tells a story that illustrates her vision in action. She was asked to do an interview on a cable TV show about health vacations as the new direction for women. In a passing conversation, the pro-ducers began talking about other areas of focus for future shows. They told Sheila they were looking for someone to do segments on reducing the stress of travel. No sooner said than done. Sheila was a natural for that job. Next, they told her they were looking at interesting things going on in California. Well, Sheila just happens to be on the board for the Ojai Music Festival. Before she knew it, they had everyone organized to come up to Ojai to do a remote taping on the festival. Then they were searching for California designers. Sheila, who is known for supporting everyone who supports her, had on an outfit which they loved, by Joan McCurry, an Ojai designer. They suggested doing a segment on Sheila and Joan together. If that wasn't enough, they wanted to know about the beads she was wearing made by Barbara Bowman, another client. By the time Sheila left the interview, six more shows were set up. Creating possibilities pays off.

One of the reasons opportunities always present themselves to Sheila is that she has her scanner operating all the time. She picks up the signals because her way of looking at the world involves bringing different elements together. What we have learned from watching Sheila is that every situation presents

opportunities. You have to be smart enough and open enough
to take advantage of them.

Another entrepreneur who does just that is Judith Sans,
president of her own cosmetic company in Atlanta. On a recent airline trip, Judith noticed the negative aura and unattractive uniforms of the flight attendants. Most other people would
have ended this experience by commenting to a friend on the
surly attitudes and ugly uniforms. But Judith doesn't know
how to do things in unobtrusive ways. She made an appointment to talk to the person in charge and gave the airline more
feedback than they probably wanted. Never one to mince
words, Judith told them, "You're turning people out of charm
school by the thousands and they look like the wrath of God."
Because Judith saw the possibilities in transforming these people, she volunteered her time to give them a class on attitude,
color, health, and nutrition to help them look and feel better.
She didn't charge them a dime. She just wanted them to see
that a physical transformation could affect their attitudes. This
airline now pays for Judith's services and has asked her to do a
video tape for them. Did Judith foresee this possibility? We'd
bet on it.

Not only does she seize opportunities, she teaches her fran-
chisees to do the same. One of her saleswomen living in a
community of 18,000 people complained to Judith that it was
difficult to rack up big sales in her small, blue-collar town.
Judith, bent on showing her the limiting effects of the assump-
tions she was making, went there and became "salesperson for
a day." Judith had $8,700 in sales to show for her one day's
work. But more illuminating is the story she tells of one family
who bought $3,400 worth of services and products.

This family of four (husband, wife, and two teenage children) wanted to build their confidence and improve their appearance. The seventeen-year-old boy had a severe case of acne
and his teenage sister was overweight and had excessive facial
hair. Judith spent a half a day with them, not just selling, but

counseling. As a result, the young girl plans to see an endocrinologist to get her hormones in balance. Judith also put her on a nutritional regimen that will help her lose weight. She set up appointments to remove facial hair and to embark on a total makeover. Was it worth the hefty price tag? This family thought so. Money that had been saved for a second car was used to make all four of them look and feel better about themselves. Judith, who feels her purpose in life is to help others feel more confident, showed this family and her franchisee the value of seeing possibilities.

Judith made another profitable connection when she combined her ability to "find a need and fill it" with her sensitivity to helping people. She knew that black, Hispanic, and oriental women were virtually ignored by the large cosmetic companies. She also knew she could help these women feel better about themselves and increase her business in the process by catering to that market. Her cosmetic company developed a "woman of color" line. Her assessment was on target. She has just sold this division to Gillette. Judith's newest venture is a cosmetic line for men. She seems to be able to catch the wave before it crests. Watch for this industry soon to develop.

How do you train your mind to function like a possibility scanner as Sheila and Judith do? One way is to take Barbara Millard's advice to learn from the person with the bird's eye view. When we interviewed Barbara she was president of Computerland.

"I would do any job to work near somebody at the top . . . I would take a lesser job; I would take lesser pay." As the daughter of William Millard, the founder of Computerland, Barbara has had that rare opportunity to learn from her dad's possibility thinking. But you don't have to be the daughter of the CEO to recognize possibilities.

Patty Matson, vice president of corporate communications at Cap Cities/ABC, told us a story that speaks for itself. When Patty was transferred to Washington, she was approached by a young man who wanted to be her secretary. She told him she already had one who would be coming in a few weeks. Undeterred, he said he would volunteer his services until Patty's secretary came on board. Even when she arrived, he continued to volunteer on a part-time basis.

When Patty moved to New York to take the job at ABC, this young man kept in touch. While Patty already had a secretary assigned in her new job, one of her subordinates had an opening. She called this young man and offered him the position even though it was low paying. He jumped at the opportunity and moved to New York to take the job. Once there, he did his usual phenomenal work and when a position opened for a researcher, he took that position . . . again, at less pay. Now this former secretary is associate producer of "Nightline."

While this story illustrates what seeing possibilities can do for a person, the next story shows what not having this ability can cost. Patty remembers a highly skilled, competent woman applying for a job commensurate with her skill and experience. Though one was not available, ABC did offer her a lower level job at lesser pay. She refused. Patty speculates that the woman's talent and the opportunities that subsequently opened in that department would have meant two promotions by now. This woman chose not to grab the possibility of getting a foot in the door as a way to leverage a better opportunity down the road. Patty understands this woman's reluctance. She cautions that taking a lower level job can have high payoff but it is risky business. There's always the danger of getting stuck in a dead-end job. To minimize the risks when an opportunity like this presents itself, she advises careful scrutiny of the company to see if it's one that, like ABC, promotes from within. If the company does, there is a very good chance that possibility seers will be rewarded.

It is clear that seeing possibilities pays big dividends. The "so what" for you is that you can develop this ability. Identify the possibility seers around you and stick to them like glue. Pay attention to how they look at the world and how they multiply the opportunities in situations. Ask them how they would expand your career or business if they were in your shoes. At first they'll probably think of a lot of ideas you hadn't thought of yourself. But after hanging around a 360-degree thinker for a while, sniffing out possibilities will become second nature. You'll know "you've arrived" when your possibility thinking matches theirs. Don't stop there. Now attach yourself to someone who creates even more ideas.

How do good ideas develop? One way is through incubation, a fermentation process when ideas are slowly mulled over, evolve, and finally take shape. They grow, generate other ideas, and make connections in seemingly unrelated ways. Incubation is critical to any creative idea and quiet time is critical to incubation. You must carve out fifteen minutes twice a day just to be still and think. We can hear the cacophony of excuses from busy people who already suffer from the "too much to do and too little time" syndrome. "Are you kidding?" they ask. "I hardly have time to go to the bathroom." "You've got to be joking. I can't even get the necessary things done, let alone thirty minutes of solitude." Our response to these protests? It may not be easy but it is mandatory if you want to become an increasingly effective, successful, and creative person. Reflection and processing time pay big dividends by offering insight and ideas that can't take shape in the stress of survival. If you want to dream up possibilities and think up solutions to problems in creative ways, then stop focusing on how difficult it will be to find the quiet time and simply create it in your schedule, like you find time to eat and sleep. Incubation produces insights and solves problems, but it demands quiet.

Without solitude, thinking is fragmented by the mundane tasks, activities, and responsibilities that frenetically fill your day. It is difficult to chauffeur kids, take the dog to the vet, navigate a career, fix dinner, go to the cleaners, and still be a self-generating idea machine. Though you are busy, sometime either early in the morning or late at night, find a block of fifteen minutes to concentrate on the exciting possibilities of your current and future ventures. The best time to do this is the twilight moments just before you fall asleep. While you are sleeping, your subconscious will work on creating possibilities from the ideas you have planted. You can further help yourself by not censoring your ideas, by keeping your mind open, and by valuing even the ludicrous notions.

Most people would subscribe to the idea that seeing possibilities is important, but the real challenge is in generating them. The first step in developing *360-Degree Vision* is valuing an open mind. This means not giving an out-of-hand rejection to new ideas, even the extreme ones. Keep learning to expand your options by watching people who create them. Create your own by being willing to indulge yourself in a rich fantasy life. Remember your visualizations mentioned earlier in this chapter. It is out of these technicolor dreams that possibilities are born.

CHUTZPAH

"Don't be afraid to take risks. Nothing is permanent. Say "yes" blindly to the question of: can you do this?"

JUDY MILLER

"If you play it safe in life, you've decided that you don't want to grow anymore."

SHIRLEY HUFSTEDLER

It's one thing to dream and fantasize. It's something else to make dreams a reality. The boldness necessary to implement these dreams has set people apart throughout history. Susan B. Anthony and her troops of suffragettes wouldn't have changed the course of history without it. Peter Ueberroth couldn't have defied financial disaster, terrorism, and grid-lock to pull off the highly successful 1984 Summer Olympic Games without it. And audacious Joan Rivers, as America's premier comedienne, wouldn't have millions of fans with dollars to match if she didn't have it, either. What is this elusive "it" they all share? In a word, *Chutzpah.* Nothing great was ever achieved without it and the dynamic, powerful, and successful women we interviewed prove this point.

What are the qualities behind this strange word? Try guts, courage, audacity. The boldness, nerve, and risk taking which are the essence of Chutzpah translate Megavisions into megarealities. Chutzpah brings a belief in self to match the epic thinking that is central to Megavision. It makes the seemingly inconceivable possible.

It's the kind of guts that Nina Blanchard, the reknowned modeling agent, showed when she faced 4 to 1 odds, chasing several young toughs out of the lobby of her Hollywood office building. Picture a short, middle-aged woman telling four streetwise hoodlums, "How dare you terrorize the women in my office. I'll cut your whatevers off!"

Chutzpah works with bosses, too. Can you imagine responding to your boss's question about whether or not he should terminate you with, "If you fire me, who will do your work?" That's what Davina Lane did and it kept her on the job at CIGNA. (We believe her then boss is now gone.)

What Nina and Davina have in common is a powerful belief in themselves that is the essence of *Chutzpah.* They show a boldness that stems from their willingness to bet on themselves. Like blue-chip stocks, they know they'll come through. Without *Chutzpah, Megavision* would remain exactly that—a big vision with no chance of becoming a reality. The women we talked with are not in the business of pipe dreams.

One woman whose boldness makes her visions a reality is Gail Koff, a partner in Jacoby and Meyers, the McDonalds of the legal profession. Gail had *Grand-Scale Thinking* and *360-Degree Vision.* But if she hadn't had the *Chutzpah* to approach Jacoby and Meyers her dream wouldn't have become a reality. When Gail made the daring proposal to them that they expand their business to provide affordable legal services to middle-class America, they had only four offices in California. Gail had a dream that coincided with theirs, to decrease the intimidation and inequity existing in the legal system. That's no easy task.

To do that, they had to have the guts to buck the legal establishment and the norms of the profession. In a field that for centuries has prohibited any form of advertising, they were the first to do such unorthodox things as advertise on television and open branches in department stores. Now, several years and 150 offices later, they are halfway toward their goal. But Gail's boldness doesn't stop with these accomplishments. She envisions products such as publications and a whole new market in servicing small businesses. In fact, she has written a book, *A Practical Guide to Law,* that makes law understandable for the lay person. Labeling herself as much an entrepreneur as a lawyer, Gail is quick to see and promote the magnitude of an idea, especially a bold one. She certainly has done so with Jacoby and Meyers.

The good news of *Chutzpah* is that it enables mere mortals to envision and accomplish Herculean feats, but it's not for the faint of heart. This kind of daring is sometimes alienating and threatening. While *Chutzpah* accomplishes results, it frequently intimidates others.

But Muriel Siebert doesn't care. In fact, she was hoping it would when she chased purse snatchers four blocks down the streets of Manhattan. Though this middle-aged woman who is in no shape to run the New York Marathon was pitted against two young thieves, she gave a healthy chase with no thought about her personal safety. Muriel readily admits this was not her smartest move. But it's exactly the kind of boldness that's gotten her where she is today.

We don't want to convey the impression that to have *Chutzpah* means to perpetually wear boxing gloves, but this feisty pioneer continually puts herself in the ring. One of her most important battles involved getting her seat on the New York Stock Exchange. No woman had done that in its 200-year history. Not only did she have to raise close to a half a million dollars for her seat, she had to get two members to sponsor her. This was not easy in an all-male bastion that had built an invincible fortress against women. When Jim O'Brien of Solomon Brothers and Hutzler sponsored her, he was not number one on the popularity poll among his male colleagues. He didn't care. This broker, who also had *Chutzpah,* had faith in Muriel's intelligence and her integrity. Together they persevered. Some of her Wall Street colleagues were even less happy when she became one of the first to offer discount brokerage fees.

Muriel continues to rewrite the story of women overcoming obstacles. She recently got a bill passed that forced the downtown luncheon clubs to open their membership to women. One of her most prized awards is a plaque from Mayor Koch commending her on this work. Muriel is unbound by norms and not afraid to do the unconventional. She is also not afraid to stand up to pressure, no matter where it comes from.

Whether or not Muriel's boldness is your style, it is clear that without the guts to stick your head above the crowd, there's very little chance of distinguishing yourself, and even less chance of success. You can dream big and see possibilities around every corner BUT UNTIL YOU HAVE THE COURAGE TO RISK DISAPPROVAL, YOUR SPHERE OF INFLUENCE WILL BE LIMITED. So will your self-esteem and your accomplishments.

Chutzpah might be uncomfortable for those of us raised with the biblical notion that the meek shall inherit the earth, and the centuries-old notion that a woman should know her place. To act with *Chutzpah* means overcoming the limitations of your early socialization. It also means feeling entitled. The women we talked with do not ask for permission from others. Being your own source of permission is an easy idea to understand. Sometimes it takes a lifetime to implement if your rearing does not reinforce strength and independence of thought. You can, however, become the source of your own entitlement by affirming your worth and your dreams.

This process works because we continually send messages about our circumstances and actions to our subconscious in the form of our thoughts and ideas. Some are positive: "This is a super job and I love the challenge." Some are negative: "I can never face the boss this morning." Affirmations are positive messages that supplant old, negative thoughts. They create new feelings of power, control, and fulfillment. "I am successful and capable," rather than "I'm not sure I can do it." These affirmations become the positive work orders sent to the subconscious to redirect our lives. They maximize our control, eliminate the victim stance, and become self-fulfilling prophecies. They build self-esteem so that you are able to take the risks that acting with *Chutzpah* requires.

If lack of entitlement is holding you back and keeping you from acting boldly, let self-affirmation work for you by following these steps:

1. Create affirmations that relate to *your* own goals. Some examples are:
     "My career is flourishing."
     "My influence is widely felt in this organization."
     "My business is growing by leaps and bounds."

2. Use the present tense because the subconscious buys the suggestion as a present reality and expends its energy on making it so. Using the future tense only reinforces the fact that the desired condition is not a present reality. Say "I am growing more successful everyday," rather than "I will be successful."

3. State affirmations in the positive. "I will not fail" reinforces the tie to failure and makes it the basis of comparison. On the other hand, saying "I am successful" suggests only the idea of success and makes no comparison with failure for the subconscious to receive.

4. Reinforce your affirmations by repeating them throughout the day. You can do this by saying them to yourself out loud, by writing them on 3 × 5 cards and reading them frequently, or by taping your affirmations on a cassette that you set aside time to listen to. Hearing your own voice talk about your dreams is a powerful influencer of your subconscious.

Affirmations will help you feel more entitled, but believing in yourself is not enough. You have to ACT on this belief and take some risks. In fact, risk taking is critical to the whole concept of *Megavision*. It's risky to think big; it's riskier to fantasize about possibilities; and it's riskiest of all to try to make these big dreams come true. You might not succeed. You might face ridicule. You might have to face your own sense of inadequacy or other people's disappointment in you. Most of us continuously wrestle with our limits, but without risk taking we don't expand them or our world. The question is, how do you get beyond the sweaty palms or butterflies in the stomach to take risks? Follow this effective two-stage process. The first step gets your *Thinking* in top risk-taking shape. The second gets your *Behavior* in prime condition.

Mental Calisthentics for Risk Taking:

1. *Perception determines risk.*

Risk lies in the eye of the beholder. One person's risk is another person's yawn. There is a true story about a tightrope walker who unhesitatingly walks between New York skyscrapers on his skinny little wire. He doesn't see this feat as risky. This same performer, who feels at home high above the city streets, shudders at the very thought of marriage. Confronting himself and another person in an intimate relationship fills him with panic. All of us, like the tightrope walker, subjectively experience and evaluate risk.

Your personality influences this subjective evaluation. People who are natural adventure seekers and pioneers will be on the frontiers of risk. They need constant stimulation and change so risk is more appealing to them. They can't help but seek it out anymore than someone who is security-minded can help holding on to the status quo. If you shy away from risk but know you need it to revitalize your life as you enlarge your vision, don't run for the safe port every time the seas get rocky. Make increased risk taking an important priority for your own growth and start by designing risk-taking increments that you can live with. Expect some discomfort. That goes with your growth. It will also be part of your exhilaration.

2. *The essence of risk taking is confronting fears.*

If your fears are not confronted, barriers to risk taking will not be overcome. There is not a person alive who hasn't experienced fear. It's as human as breathing. Who hasn't been intimidated by the fear of being rejected or looking foolish? Who hasn't, at one time or another, had sleepless nights worrying about appearing incompetent or dealing with financial insecurity? What these fears have in common is that they can hold you back and are usually worse than the reality. To get beyond them, face your ogres. Once met, eyeball to eyeball in the light of day, these monsters lose their power. Ask yourself what's the worst thing that would happen if someone said "no" to you or laughed at you. Would your life really be over if you lost your job? (It might be just the kick in the pants you need to take a necessary risk.)

The truth is we've all had painful times worrying about our fears but we live through these rough periods. When you can deal with the worst, you're home free. Confronting your fears puts you in charge and gives you back your power.

3. *The biggest risk may be not risking.*

Missed opportunities are a huge loss because you never know what might have been. Don't make your life living testimony to "The Road Not Taken." When you do a risk analysis, make sure your ledger accounts for not only the potential loss in taking the risk but also the potential loss in NOT taking the risk.

Irene Cohen, president of her own personnel agency, warns that women are limited by their unwillingness to incur big debt (by her definition, in the millions). She advises, "Once you've built a successful company, don't be afraid of 'mega-success,' even if it means taking on greater debt." Chuckling, she admits that in her current business expansion, she is still financing the growth herself. Irene would advise women to do what she says, not what she does. Be courageous enough to risk other people's money on your own venture.

Behavioral Exercises for Risk Taking:

1. Ask for help.

Chutzpah isn't built in a day. It grows step by step, so take your first steps now. The next time you need assistance in any aspect of your career, don't sit in a corner waiting to be discovered. Think of some influential people who might be helpful. Once you know what information you'd like, contact these individuals. What have you got to lose? If you receive no acknowledgment or a rejection, you're no worse off than you are right now. If they respond, there's no telling what this contact can do, directly or indirectly, to enhance your career. The future belongs to those who are appropriately BOLD. Start becoming more so, NOW.

2. Be honest and direct in your dealings with all people.

While this behavior should be as natural as breathing, it isn't. Instead, it is rare, unconventional, and audacious. We are not suggesting brutal, ruthless honesty. We are suggesting the following. The next time you are dissatisfied with either goods or services you purchase, say something—not to your friends or colleagues—but to the provider. The challenge is to be direct and honest in a firm but unstrident way. When you are displeased with someone's actions, be daring and tell them. Just remember to be specific about behaviors, non-threatening in tone and clear about what you'd like instead. You can also be just as direct about positive feedback.

3. Enroll in the risk a week club.

The only membership fee is a spiral note pad on which you can record your risks and the outcomes. Consider risks you might take by pinpointing where your life feels limited. What are you afraid of? If it's rejection, when you meet someone new, extend your hand first. If it's fear of financial insecurity, challenge yourself to invest or buy something that you've longed for. The important thing is to see you can survive rejection and that spending money doesn't leave you destitute. If you're dissatisfied at work, make an appointment with your boss. Ask for that raise, make that proposal, or request specific changes that would make your job more satisfying. By taking one risk a week you will gain the confidence you need to take bold action and see outstanding results.

Risk taking is many things . . . scary, exhilarating, growth producing, and intimidating. Above all, it is imperative if you are going to have the kind of *Chutzpah* that brings your *Megavisions* to life.

Megavision stands apart from the other four success factors. They help you arrive at your destination but Megavision gives it form and substance. It's the map that charts your course. It emerges from a belief that things can get better, that options are limitless, and that progress is attainable. Everyone has parts of *Megavision* to some degree, but it only becomes a truly potent force when you successfully combine *Grand-Scale Thinking, 360-Degree Vision* and *Chutzpah.* That terrific threesome, the desire to make a huge impact, the ability to create options, and the daring to bring them about, make you a force with which to be reckoned.

6
NO EXCUSES, JUST RESULTS

"Nobody makes you do anything. You do it to yourself."

CAROLE MORTON

There was no shortage of excuses if our interviewees wanted to use them. They simply would not allow these potential excuses to be their reasons for not succeeding.

Having dyslexia, a learning disability that made reading difficult, did not keep Ernesta Ballard Barnes, formerly Regional Administrator of the EPA and currently president of Pacific Celebration '89, from learning voraciously, being a quick study, and eventually becoming one of the highest-ranking women in government.

Being one of ten female law students in a class of five hundred and fifteen at Harvard in the early 1960s meant Congresswoman Pat Schroeder saw some men in her class change their seats rather than sit next to a woman. She didn't let that discrimination thwart her career.

Being refused a $5,000 business loan without a husband's signature because bankers were afraid she might get pregnant and default on her loan didn't stop Judith Sans from using her entrepreneurial talent. She built a highly successful cosmetic business without that money.

Experiencing a near-fatal allergic reaction to food additives didn't stop Sandy Gooch from making her mark in the world of nutrition. Rather than being stopped by her illness, Sandy built a thriving business helping others avoid her problem.

These resilient survivors, like the others we interviewed, have no intention of relying on excuses. They have every intention of producing results. The statement that best reflects this results-oriented behavior comes from Tom Justice, a colleague of ours, who says "You can have it *or* all the reasons you don't have it." His aphorism, which so aptly expresses the essense of the *No Excuses, Just Results* orientation, is lived by these women who have found a way to have what they want, rather than hide behind the reasons.

Collectively, the 100 women we interviewed faced most of the problems human beings experience in a lifetime. Their travails may look a lot like some of yours. They have survived divorces, functioned as single parents, experienced difficulties in raising capital for business start-ups, nurtured careers and families at the same time, and found doors closed because of discrimination against women. Beyond this garden variety list of difficulties, some of our interviewees faced extraordinarily painful times—being orphaned or losing a parent in childhood, growing up in unstable homes due to parent's mental and physical illness, and surviving the death of their own children. The difference between these durable survivors and those who fare less well is that they refused to use these obstacles as reasons for not achieving their goals.

This *No Excuses, Just Results* approach to life is not only what makes these women so inspirational, it is what makes them so successful. As corny as it sounds, these undeterred professional women are the embodiment of the cliché "where there's a will, there's a way." They show the power of an iron will coupled with a pragmatic, problem-solving approach to obstacles as they deflect troubles to get beyond life's immovable objects. Whiners and complainers won't be found among these winners. They possess a potent combination of optimism and realism. They see life's roadblocks clearly; they just make sure the barriers are temporary by finding ways around them.

The *No Excuses, Just Results* approach to life combines two inseparable parts. The first is an attitude that shows the relentless determination of trailblazing pioneers. They won't be stopped. The second is a problem-solving mentality that sees life's difficulties as a series of Rubic's cubes. These women figure out a way to solve the puzzle. This chapter will show you how to develop both the determined attitude and the problem-solving mentality by helping you come to grips with your self-sabotaging excuses and by showing you how to see obstacles as opportunities to seize success. But before you can have a fully developed *No Excuses, Just Results* attitude, you have to know your excuses.

EXCUSITIS: THE TOXIC DISEASE

"Defeat is a wonderful opportunity for learning. I've learned my best lessons through defeat."

LaRae Orullian

KNOw Excuses

Excuses—we've all heard them, we've all used them. Try hard as we can, the two of us can come up with only one real benefit to using them. They sometimes serve as social amenities that save face. For example, you may not want to have lunch with an individual whom you find offensive. It is kinder to say, "I can't meet with you. I have a pressing deadline," than to say, "Lunch with you would be irrelevant because being in your company makes me lose my appetite."

These kinds of "little lie" excuses are not harmful to you if you are not deceiving yourself while you spare the feelings of another person. However, they are dangerous when you use them to fool yourself. These deadly excuses give you rationalizations for your lack of accomplishment. We've all been guilty of making excuses from time to time. It's not difficult to do since there's usually an endless supply of conditions around which we can build them. They give us permission to achieve far below our potential while still winning approval. But like a house of cards, these pretexts for not living up to your capability won't stand.

Here are some of the most frequent ones we hear. Do you recognize yourself or anyone you know in these statements? What's your reaction to them?

—I can't go back to school because I have kids to send to college.

—I can't focus on a career right now because I have little kids at home.

—I can't go back to school because I'm too old.

—I can't start my own business because I don't have the start-up capital.

—I can't look for a new job because I'd have to take a salary cut and lose benefits.

—It's pointless to ask my boss for what I want because I'll never get it.

—There's no use confronting my employee because he/she will never change anyway.

—I can't leave my spouse, no matter how bad the marriage, until our kids are out of the house.

The conditions that provoke the excuses are real. Young children do need care and college educations do need to be paid for. We are not quarreling with the fact that these obstacles exist; we are quarreling with the use of them as reasons for not pursuing your stated dreams. Scratch the surface of any successful person and you'll find a myriad of reasons that could have prevented her from succeeding. But obstacles have power only if you allow them to.

The Two Sides of Excusitis: Seducer and Saboteur

If excuses are so damaging, why are they so prevalent? In a word, comfort. Because they give us a deceptive feeling of security, we hang on to them. They make us feel better even though they are our undoing. Let's take a look at the perverse psychological payoffs we get from making excuses. These temporary benefits are the sources of their seductive and destructive power.

1. The "I Told You So" Syndrome

Heading the top of most people's feel-good list is being right. Human beings have a strong subconscious need to be correct that sometimes conflicts with their conscious need to be happy. Having our view of the world validated is an aphrodisiac. Excuses do that for us. Watch out, though, if your pattern has been to create disappointment and defeat. Since the need to feel right is addictive, the excuse becomes a negative self-fulfilling prophecy. If you believe you'll never get a loan to start that new business you've longed for, the first refusal you get will prove you right. Then you'll pat yourself on the back while you sing a resounding chorus of "I told you so" instead of going to a second, third, or even tenth bank until you finally get your loan. The problem is that the benefit of being right is minimal when compared with the cost of setting yourself up for defeat. All the time you are feeling self-righteous, your dreams are turning to ashes.

2. The "Poor Me" Syndrome

Feeling like "poor me" brings us attention and sympathy from others. The pity we get may feel comforting. More to the point, it may get us what we want from people motivated by guilt. However, it is also a saboteur that undermines us. It demeans us by making us the impotent victims of outside forces. It reinforces powerlessness, not an entirely foreign feeling to women. For example, as long as you tell yourself that you aren't being promoted because you are a woman, you will spend your energy feeling sorry for yourself instead of figuring out what you can do to advance your career.

3. The "You Can't Fight City Hall" Syndrome

The sense of futility reflected in this mentality releases us from the responsibility to take action and from the distasteful job of pitting our wits against an unresponsive system. It gives you permission to "cop out." The freedom from responsibility comes at an exhorbitant cost—control in your own life. Like a tumbleweed, you are abandoning yourself to the mercy of the elements.

4. The "It's Not My Fault" Syndrome

This is the loophole with the capital L. It frees us from accountability and means we don't have to come through on our commitments to ourselves or others. Energy that could be spent on accomplishing a goal is spent on deflecting the blame and finger pointing.

"Look to yourself rather than others for opportunity."
MARTHA GONZALEZ MIKITA

Excusitis is self-inflicted; it can be self-cured. Once you understand the gains and losses from perpetuating excusitis, you can find a way to remedy it. The first way to start eradicating this dread disease is to confront your own excuses. What reasons are you giving yourself for not doing some of the things you say you want to do? Equally important, what are you gaining from hanging on to these excuses?

Once you understand your answers to the last two questions, it's time to determine your true priorities. Do you say you want to go back to school because your boss, spouse, or friends think you should, when in fact, you're satisfied doing exactly what you are doing? Do you talk about a promotion because all the magazine articles you read tell you that successful women are all on a fast track even though you love your present job? Stop and look at what you really want to do. Then you can make active choices, not defensive excuses. You may decide you want to remain a supervisor so you can have some job responsibility while saving time for other things that matter to you. That is a more powerful position than complaining you can't take a crack at a promotion because you have young children at home who need your time.

The second remedy for curing excusitis is to admit the excuses that you're using and be honest about what they give you. While being right might feel good to you temporarily, is it more important to you than being successful? Even though sympathy is soothing when you get it, is it more vital to you in the long run than respect?

If you've made the decision to shed your excuses, you may face a different kind of obstacle—other people's resentment. The success and fulfillment you achieve when you do so will produce hostility and disapproval from those who are still hanging on to their excuses. Don't run scared from their intimidation. Your own success will be a healthy and satisfying reward but you will have to deal with the fact that, however unintentionally, you've become a mirror forcing others to confront their own justifications for not accomplishing.

Marilyn Barnewall tells us a story that illustrates this sometimes painful phenomenon. When Marilyn was made the first female vice president at the United Bank of Denver, she remembers thinking this promotion would be great, not only for her, but for other women. As Marilyn tells it, that's not quite what happened. "I suddenly found out that the other women resented me because I had removed their excuses for not achieving. They had been saying 'Why should I work hard? I can't get ahead because they don't have women V.P.'s in this bank anyway.' Then suddenly they had one and they said, 'Damn you. I don't have an excuse anymore.' It was very lonely and very painful."

Difficult though it might be, the women we talked with aren't done in by other people's disapproval or life's obstacles. If you are going to realize your dreams, you, too, will have to learn not to let people or circumstances hinder you. The power of this *No Excuses, Just Results* attitude can be seen in the making of Nina Blanchard's successful model agency. Nina's life is a smorgasbord of would-be excuses. Look at just a few she could have used: Poverty, crippling illness, career disappointment, discrimination, and a failed marriage. But this woman who believes that we each control our own destiny would not be deterred.

Nina had already shown her determination and resilience by overcoming polio at age sixteen. As an aspiring seventeen-year-old actress with the grand sum of thirty-seven dollars in her pocket, she headed east to the Big Apple to launch her career. Not finding the hoped-for success, she worked first as a copywriter, then as a makeup artist, and finally as a casting director for NBC where she met her future husband. Because of his job, they moved back to Los Angeles where, lo and behold, she met another obstacle. Women weren't allowed to be makeup artists for the studios. As if all those difficulties weren't enough, a few years later her marriage crumbled and she separated from her husband. Shortly thereafter she was widowed. But Nina didn't have time to feel sorry for herself.

She went from penniless to bankrupt when her own modeling school franchise failed. Desperate, she borrowed $300 and a "hole in the wall" office from a friend to begin her own agency with a few inexperienced models. The borrowed funds spent on a brochure featuring her models worked. When calls from photographers and advertisers began coming in a few days after her mailing, the Nina Blanchard Agency was launched. Now, twenty-five years later, it is the biggest on the West Coast and one of the top agencies in the nation.

Most of us would be hard-pressed to out-obstacle Nina. The only thing she had on her side was her guts. But that kind of courage is not an *Only.* In fact, it proved to be the deciding factor in building her modeling empire.

There were plenty of reasons for Nina to give up, but she wouldn't allow any of them to give her an out. If you want to be successful, you, too, need to bar the doors, barricade the windows, and not give yourself a way out. As Marilyn Barnewall puts it, "Everything you do in life is a matter of choice. Until you learn that, you're always going to take a cop-out, you're always going to find a convenient excuse for not doing something. The problem is that most people think you're going to have a good choice and a bad choice. Successful people understand how to pick the best of two bad choices based on the alternatives." And they don't let either obstacles or fears hold them back. Marilyn goes on to say, "I watched a tape of *Gone with the Wind.* Everyone kept saying Scarlet wasn't afraid of anything. She was afraid of everything! She just didn't let it stop her."

We hope we've touched a few of your nerves as we've discussed excuses. If you found yourself saying "guilty" on several occasions, then the following tips will help you block your own escape routes.

Tips

1. Pay attention to the words you use. Omit words like "can't" and "yes, but" from your vocabulary. Just using them makes excusitis part of your mentality and makes you impotent. You also give away power when you use phrases such as "they won't" and "I have no choice." The truth is, you *always* have a choice and using phrases such as "I choose to" and "I've made a decision to" give you power in your own life.

2. Keep people around you who make it difficult for you to deceive yourself. They are the quintessential question askers who don't let you hide behind your excuses without at least admitting them to yourself so that you eventually make an active choice. A colleague of ours, Natasha Josefowitz, says in her book *Paths to Power* that we all need three kinds of support from the people in our lives—we need a shoulder to cry on, a brain to pick, and a kick in the pants! This last one is critical to developing the *No Excuses* mentality. Make a contract with colleagues and friends you trust not to collude with you to deceive yourself.

RESULTS: THE BOTTOM LINE

"You can't legislate equality. If you want it, you'd better jolly well go out there, work hard, and prove yourself."

ARLENE MEEKER

For these women, achievement is the measure of success. This achievement has many faces—balance sheets covered in black ink, influence that cuts a wide swath, businesses whose growth continues to mushroom, and meaningful changes in society brought about by their tireless resolve. You don't hear them complaining, you just see them doing. They let their actions speak for them and when they do, they have the E. F. Hutton effect—everybody listens. These results-oriented women know that the proof is in the pudding. They don't waste their energy complaining about injustice, wallowing in problems or railing about prejudice. Instead, they use their talent and their initiative to "deliver the goods." These triumphant achievers are masters of R&R: REALISM and RESILIENCE. They are pragmatic realists in assessing the terrain. They know that to bring about what ought to be they first have to deal with what is. They understand the economic, political, and social realities of the world.

Realism: Dealing with What Is

Judy Miller, whose job as vice president of marketing at Braun and Company requires much international travel, comes face to face with these realities regularly. One of her most intriguing experiences occurred when she went to Saudi Arabia to arrange logistics for a trip where heads of state were meeting. Judy planned to spend four days making sure details were taken care of and that the meetings would flow smoothly. Unbeknown to her, the Saudi government, wanting to maintain secrecy at these high level talks, closed all roads and airspace. Judy was not permitted to leave. Her four-day trip turned into almost a month. She had outfits and pantyhose for four days. Because she was sequestered, she could get no more. She ended up washing her hose nightly, and toward the end her last pair had two quarter-size holes in them which she resorted to taping. Judy didn't complain about conditions, she just dealt with them and could even laugh about her situation.

In addition to showing Judy's kind of realistic attitude, our interviewees also understand the plain facts about human nature. Facing life head-on forearms these determined professionals in their battle to clear obstacles from their path. For example, both Barbara Millard, daughter of Computerland's founder William Millard, and Christie Hefner, daughter of Playboy magnate Hugh Hefner, recognized that their promotions to the top of their respective organizations would cause a stir. Cries of nepotism were heard. Christie and Barbara were discounted by numerous observers who viewed their appointments as proof positive of the "who you know" theory of rising to the top. Their relationships with their fathers as well as their youth and attractiveness blocked some people from seeing the skill, intelligence, and competence these women brought to their work. Rather than complaining or being defensive, they hit the credibility issue head-on and won people over.

Barbara was not afraid to deal with this issue. In fact, she raised it herself in our interview, acknowledging not just her rare opportunity but her own competence as well. While she admits that she might not be sitting in that chair if her father weren't the founder, she knows that she would be doing something important. As a twenty-eight-year-old president who has been accused of getting her position because of her father, she is used to the testing.

She went through a particularly difficult time when her company became embroiled in a legal battle with Micro/Vest. Herbert Hafif, Micro/Vest's attorney, had always been openly critical of William Millard's management in general and his decision to make Barbara president specifically. Before meeting her, Hafif is quoted in an L.A. *Times* article as saying, "How in the hell any twenty-seven-year-old daughter of some rich guy could have any intrinsic abilities was beyond me."

After meeting Barbara and working with her in her new position as manager of the legal case against Micro/Vest, he changed his tune. Hafif said that Barbara ". . . more than anyone else, convinced me that the defendants are worthy of the trust of my clients in extending the bond." About his change of heart, Hafif said in the same article, "I'm embarrassed to be saying this because people might think I've been had. I'd like to think that I'm not too set in my ways to acknowledge a misjudgment or two, and I certainly misjudged her abilities."

Barbara and Christie show the realism that is typical of these successful women. To our questions about problems women face in a man's world, we heard astounding examples of the prejudices these women have dealt with in their careers. Their stories create a catalogue of realities faced and obstacles overcome.

> "People will react to your being a woman. Don't lower your sights. It passes."
>
> PAT SCHROEDER

• CLAIRE ROTHMAN, vice president of the Forum, remembers when her then boss Jack Kent Cooke told her, "You're the best in the business and I pay you the least." As the only woman in the country running a major sports/entertainment facility, Claire remembers feeling robbed of her dignity.

• SUSAN HAGER, president of the Washington, D.C., PR firm of Hager, Sharp and Abramson, recalls one of her early high level negotiations with a client. She was startled by a question from one of the men present who interrupted the business discussion to ask bluntly, "Who's taking care of your child?"

• JUDITH RUNSTAD, a partner in the Seattle law firm of Foster, Pepper and Riviera, went to Washington as a summer clerk for a United States senator. When she got there, this Phi Beta Kappa who had graduated with honors at the top of her class was led to a typewriter with the other women while all

the men were led into the senator's offices to discuss committee assignments.

• JILL WINE-BANKS, deputy attorney general of the state of
Illinois, was the first woman in the criminal division of the
Department of Justice. For two years during Watergate, Jill
was so visible that she felt she could not make a mistake because she knew the men were watching her. This didn't surprise her but what did was Jeb Magruder's lawyer's request
that she fetch some coffee.

• GRACE DAVIS, deputy mayor of the City of Los Angeles,
remembers when she was a biology student at UCLA. Her
professor told her that girls belonged in the kitchen and not in
the lab. Her professor also recognized reality when he told
Grace, "I can't keep you out because it's a public university."

In spite of these anachronistic examples of stone age thinking, the women with whom we talked don't see themselves as
victims of discrimination, nor do they lament their plight.
They would understand Mayor Dianne Feinstein's belief that
the biggest problems facing women in business today are 1.
being taken seriously and 2. surviving the testing they go
through. What has helped the mayor survive the testing is
recognizing it is there and knowing it is part of the territory.
She says, in her matter-of-fact way, "If you're going to cross
frontiers, there will be ice, sleet, snow, and jagged rocks in the
way. If you let it make you bitter, you'll never be effective."
From her own experience, the mayor understands that it's
hard not to take discrimination personally, but she sees the
reality of the double standard. While she doesn't like it and is
doing her part to change that reality, she doesn't let it stop her
or make her bitter.

"If they discourage you, they win."

JANICE JONES

Maryles Casto could have been bitter when her sterling performance was not enough to offset her gender and she was refused a management position. Coming from the Philippines, Maryles began in a small travel agency with three people. By the time she left, it had grown to thirty. While she worked very hard, the man who owned the agency refused to make her a manager because she was a woman, but that didn't stop her. She had the confidence and the pragmatism to start her own business. This dynamo, who has transformed a $500,000 a year business into over $30 million, knows that success in business comes from pragmatically figuring out how to get something done, not complaining about why you can't. Her staff is schooled in the "Don't tell me why you can't, tell me how you can" theory. They come to Maryles armed with several plans of attack to solve the problems they encounter.

Note the power of this kind of mentality. The idea that she couldn't become a manager because she was a woman, while frustrating, only served as a catalyst that propelled her into a much more satisfying and successful venture. What on the surface seemed a negative experience was converted to a positive force in her life. Maryles now thrives on her growing business and on a hard won but satisfying sense of personal power and effectiveness.

When a person has this realistic, pragmatic view of life, she recognizes that there is good news and bad news in all situations. Centuries ago, Epictetus said, "I am upset, not by events but rather by the way I view them." In twentieth-century jargon, Sam Keen, a northern California psychologist says, "What you see is what you get. Change your eyes." Seeing reality in this dispassionate way allows you to capitalize on the positive and minimize the negative in any situation. Appreciation of the two-sided coin is particularly relevant to the double standard women face in business. These successful professionals even have a positive way to look at the position of women in the male-dominated world of business. It is true that they faced barriers because of their gender. It is equally true that being a woman opened doors for them, as well. Many see their femininity as an aid, not a cross to bear.

These enterprising individuals realize they have a unique opportunity as women. PR entrepreneur Betsy Berkhemer-Credaire shares a typical reaction. "Being a woman is an added benefit. As a saleswoman, you can get in almost any door. You can finagle your way in, sometimes better than a man can."

Another case in point is Shirley Hufstedler, a giant in the legal profession. When discussing her appointment (at that time, only the second woman) to the federal court of appeals, she says matter of factly that being a woman was an advantage. Fifteen years ago when she was appointed, there was heavy political pressure to appoint qualified women to the bench. How important a factor her gender was in her appointment we don't know. What we do know is that gender wouldn't have been enough. She is supremely competent and considered brilliant in her field. Her realistic viewpoint is evident when she says, "Women have been doing broken field running for years. No one would let them go down the middle."

Not to be outdone as a pragmatist is Carol Sheppard, president of Shop 'n Chek in Atlanta. On the wall of her office is a picture that is striking, not because of its size but because of its content. There sits young, blond, female Carol in the midst of a dozen or so traditional, conservative businessmen. When asked about the picture, Carol said she had been asked to serve on the board of Decatur Bank in Atlanta. The president of the board went out of his way to assure her that she was not asked to serve as a token female but because she had made a significant contribution to the community and the industry. Unsolicited, he told Carol they needed her expertise and knowledge, not a token. But pragmatic Carol didn't care why she was asked. She was confident she would make a contribution and learn in the process. Had she been a token, that wouldn't have bothered her. The question she put to Lee shows Carol's strong sense of realism. "What is a token? It can be a coin to get you across the bridge." Carol's practical attitude, so reflective of the outlook of the other women with whom we talked, has served our interviewees well.

Some people shun pragmatism because they think it means giving up their idealism and all the fun. However, being pragmatic in facing obstacles gives an equanimity and emotional neutrality critical to getting through highly charged situations. Not being emotionally derailed by obstacles does not mean our interviewees have become jaded. They're just able to be more discriminating in where they demonstrate their passion and more detached and objective in dealing with a problem. They bring to the situation what men have historically been given accolades and promotions for—cool, unemotional logic. This realistic thinking makes it possible for them to turn a problem into an opportunity.

Resilience: The Phoenix Syndrome

> "You have to be able to handle defeat and come back from
> it. To be successful, you have to have a bit of the Phoenix in
> you."
>
> DIANNE FEINSTEIN

Bouncing back is their knee-jerk response. Like the inflatable wibbie doll, they cannot be knocked off their feet. And they've all had a lot to bounce back from. Whether it's total defeat or a temporary barrier, they react with a solution. Like the Phoenix, they rise from the ashes. Conky Johnston, President of Johnston's Foods, showed us the *Phoenix Syndrome* in action. Conky learned a lesson from a presentation she made at Alpha Beta, a large supermarket chain in the West when she attempted to get them to distribute her product. Conky remembers, "I knocked myself out. I had put together a presentation I was so proud of. I went in there and made my pitch. The buyer said, 'Conky, that's the best presentation I've ever heard in my life, but I can't buy.' " The buyer told her he had no shelf space.

Conky recalls feeling physically reduced in height when she heard the "no." "As I drove away, I was so slumped down that I could barely see over the car. I got to the signal and I determined I was not going to let Alpha Beta have my whole day. This defeat was pretty serious and I had a right to indulge in self-pity, but I decided to time it. This was worth a good five-minute downer. It was hard to look at my watch as I drove so I said that it would be three signals. When I had gone through three signals, I did something physical. I spent two hours in the Alpha Beta stores in that area, looking for a solution. I called this guy back on the phone, even though you're not supposed to call again for six weeks. First of all, he felt bad that he'd said no. Second, he was surprised I called. I said, 'Larry, I've got to come right back in. I've got the answer.' I went back, told him where he could get the extra shelf space for my product, and we got the business. If I had allowed that depression to soak me up, it [her victory] never would have happened."

Conky was able to take defeat and convert it to a victory because she first of all acknowledged and dealt with her feelings of rejection and disappointment. Then she separated herself from these feelings, and, finally, she approached the impasse as a problem to be solved. Once she eliminated her frustration and disappointment, she was able to ask herself the most important question: What can I do about it? Then she did it.

Conky has company in Lane Nemeth and Janice Jones. Adversity doesn't get them down because their determination wins out. One of the most extraordinary rises from what almost was ashes is the story of Lane Nemeth and Discovery

Toys. This former day-care center teacher started her own toy company when she couldn't find sound, safe, durable educational toys for her daughter, Tara. Her company, which last year racked up sales of $40 million, was on the brink of disaster more times than Lane would care to remember. The problems of moving into a larger warehouse, being overstocked, understocked, and sending duplicate orders as they rapidly grew, nearly brought the company to its knees, but never its founder. At one point, this determined entrepreneur made a decision that could only spread glee among business school professors using the case study method. Lane took out a business loan at 27.5 percent interest to keep her company afloat. If that weren't bad enough, she had a $7,000 prepayment penalty. Despite the harsh terms, it worked. Discovery Toys is alive and well.

On another occasion, when this tenacious and confident woman was close to bankruptcy, she staged a sit-in. The setting was not a university campus over some highly principled but distant world issue. Rather, it was the loan officer's quarters where Lane refused to leave until her loan was approved. On the verge of bankruptcy, Lane's back was against the wall. So was the banker's when she told him, "I'm going to sit here and you can call the cops. I'll even call the media, but I'm not leaving. You will not put me under." The battle wasn't easy but victory was hers. Lane's intense determination proved that you can fight city hall and win. Her "city hall" was the SBA, but who cares? Bureaucracy is bureaucracy is bureaucracy.

"Attitude is more important than aptitude."

KATHLEEN CONNELL

Janice Jones would applaud Lane's tenacity. Having it in abundance herself, she has accomplished the extraordinary, too. Five years ago, she started Chartwell and Company, a venture management firm which now boasts assets with a mar-

ket value of $15 million. But her educational background was
not in finance. She entered Wall Street through a back door,
when as a graduate student in psychology, she invested her
$4,000 student loan in stocks. She was clever enough to gener-
ate interest in a stock that was rarely traded. In fact, her dollar
a share stocks went to $88 a share. Noticing the surge of vol-
ume in his company's stock, Norman Haber arranged to meet
Janice, the lady responsible, and offered her a job. That was
her baptism on Wall Street.

It wasn't all sweetness and light. This petite blond, then in
her early twenties, was storming an all-male bastion. She still
has the scars to prove it. But as one looks at the success of
Chartwell, the last laugh is hers. Janice remembers, "Wall
Street really takes a toll on you. You have to have an iron
stomach and steel insides. I used to waste years sitting and
having luncheons with people that had absolutely no intention
of doing business with me. Hours of breakfasts, luncheons, and
dinners that went on for six or seven years! The president of
one firm on Wall Street said to me, 'You know, you've been
coming in for eight years now. I finally decided that you must
be serious.' Can you imagine, eight years and he would never
do business with me? There were times I wanted to pop the
guy. This is the kind of stamina women have to have. The
answer in the end is just wearing everyone out. I'm convinced.
In the end everyone becomes exhausted and you're still there."
Janice realizes this kind of resilience is costly, nevertheless, she
advises it. "No matter how long it takes and no matter how
many times you get knocked over, you must pick yourself up
and dust yourself off."

That resilience combined with a fix-it mentality is pervasive
among these women. Problem solving is their automatic reaction to obstacles. While there are variations on a theme, there
is a basic problem solving sequence that works for them. Their
matter-of-fact approach to problems is not earth-shattering. It

just works. They use a simple five-step process that can work for anybody.

1. *Identify the Problem*

This is the most critical aspect of the process because an incorrectly defined problem will lead to a useless solution. A foolproof method for recognizing problems is what we call "The OH-OH Symptom": Objective + Obstacle = Problem. How do you know you have a problem? Because you have a goal and something is preventing you from achieving it. This was the case for Henrietta Holsman, president of Stockton Wire, who thought she had a growing company. Expansion and growth were her goals when the Oh-Oh Symptom struck. Her objective was no longer growth; it became survival when her general manager defected to the competition. To make matters worse, he left with five people and trade secrets. Clearly, Henrietta had a problem.

2. *Analyze and Assess the Problem*

Break the problem into its component parts. Then determine which aspects you control, and which you don't. Finally, target the areas you can do something about. In Henrietta's case, she clearly had no control over people who had left or secrets that had been given to her competitors. What she did have control over was hiring new staff, reorganizing her company, and making her time available to focus on the problem. She canceled a trip to Europe and concentrated on other aspects she could control.

3. *Generate Creative Solutions*

Open your mind to a no-holds-barred brainstorming session. The more ludicrous the ideas, the better at this point. This is how breakthrough solutions are generated and the most creative, effective solutions are embedded in the seemingly ridiculous notions. Some ideas Henrietta might have generated are: 1. a "friendly" takeover of her competitor, 2. abandoning her company, 3. becoming general manager herself, 4. hiring her next-door neighbor for the position, 5. driving around her neighborhood recruiting with a megaphone, 6. raiding the competition for talent, and 7. hiring the Goodyear blimp to advertise for a merger partner. As ridiculous as these ideas may seem, embedded in them are the critical issues involved in Henrietta's dilemma—her role in the company, its personnel, and the future structure of this organization in temporary crisis.

4. *Formulate a Plan of Attack*

Decide which solutions are workable and integrate them into a plan. Had Henrietta surveyed these creative ideas, she might have decided a joint venture or merger was desirable but not with her competitor. Or she might have focused on hiring people and deciding where to put the word out as she advertises for the best candidates. In reality, Henrietta chose to interview four people, one of whom was from the competitor. She worked her plan masterfully. She did such a good selling job that all four people wanted the position.

5. *Take Action*

Determine what you're going to do, then do it. There is no substitute for action. In Henrietta's case, she interviewed and selected the applicant she thought was most honest and best-suited to her company and she's been more than satisfied with the outcome.

The best way to see results in your own life is to apply this problem-solving process when the "OH-OH" Symptom strikes. We suggest that you take a thorny problem you are currently wrestling with. Start by asking yourself what your objectives are and what obstacles you are facing. Zero in on those obstacles over which you have control and don't fritter away time and energy where it doesn't matter. Listen to Janice Jones and "Don't push water uphill." Put your energy where change is possible.

Once you know what you can change, foster creative solutions by not polarizing your choices into either-or's. Avoid "Should I or shouldn't I?" questions which generally lead to yes-no answers and either-or choices. Rather, ask "How" and "What" questions. Challenge yourself to think of at least ten solutions, from the most traditional to the highly unconventional, then combine the strengths of each. One more suggestion regarding idea generation—the more time you allow the problem to incubate, the better your potential solution will be. This means suspending judgment until you've mulled over a whole spectrum of suggestions. We know this suspension may be difficult because people generally don't like ambiguity and the feeling of being in limbo, but the short-term discomfort will be worth the long-term benefit of a more effective solution. Combine elements of the different ideas that you see as workable. Integrate them into one plan and make a time-line with specific dates, times, places, and strategies. Without these specifics, you'll have a hollow plan. Then act. Now it's time to put your money where your mouth is. All the analyzing in the world won't change anything unless you do.

In order to get the results you want in your life, you have to desire success, happiness, and joy more than you want to hang on to the reasons for not having them. Unlike our natural resources, which are exhaustable, excuses are infinite. There is a limitless supply of reasons and conditions that can thwart your ambitions. We assume that because you are reading this book, you want to have results rather than excuses and we're here to tell you that it's possible if you do a few key things:

1. Confront your excuses. Above all, make sure you never lie to yourself. Admit and accept your true priorities. Maybe the security of a steady income and a comfortable job is more enticing than the excitement and opportunity of starting your own business. Fine. Just make sure that the decision is an active choice about your career, not an excuse to abdicate responsibility for your life.

2. If you know excuses are sabotaging your success and you'd like to shed them, the best way we know to begin is by answering two questions: First, what are you getting from holding on to these excuses? Once you've come up with an answer to the first question, see if you'd like to make some changes. If you would, then answer the second one. What are you going to do about the situation you'd like to change? (Complaining isn't an option.)

3. Treat obstacles as opportunities and challenges at best, and minor hurdles at worst. Make a pact with yourself to limit the griping time. After the set period, quit complaining and take action.

4. Success is the best revenge. Don't let defeat get you down. Let it be a catalyst for releasing your inner Phoenix and watch your success rise.

5. The final P.S. is problem solve. If you want results, you're going to have to come up with solutions to the problems life will continue to throw your way.

The message from the chorus of 100 is clear. Don't take no for an answer. These women haven't and look what it's gotten them—results that have brought them satisfaction, joy, and success by their own definitions. Approaching life with a *No Excuses, Just Results* attitude means you, too, can enjoy these rewards.

7
PRACTICAL MAGIC

The women from whom we learned so much are modern-day alchemists who creatively combine old elements in new ways to produce their own brand of gold. In so doing, they weave *Practical Magic,* the fifth quality. It is a collection of business and interpersonal strategies and techniques that generates magical results. It involves an extraordinary use of uncommon, common sense. *Practical Magic* is a meshing of *Business Savvy, People Wizardry,* and a voracious appetite for *Learning.* If you are a person who has ambition, vision, and a positive attitude, this potent triple-header gives you the *"How-Tools"* to fashion your own success reality. Let's take a quick look at the components of *Practical Magic* in action.

> First-class leadership understands the culture of the institution and weaves their own issues in.
>
> DONNA SHALALA

Business Savvy, the first aspect of *Practical Magic,* involves shrewd strategizing and a non-frontal approach to problem solving. It shows itself in the kind of clever thinking that

Kathy Keeton used when she was working in London selling advertising for *Penthouse*. She had trouble getting her foot in the door to talk to potential clients, but she found a way to get their attention. She caught them off guard when she dispatched the material, not by telex or express mail, but in dogs' mouths. Her canine couriers delivered on two counts—the material reached its destination and the technique got results.

The second part of *Practical Magic* is *People Wizardry,* relationship building that fosters loyalty and commitment. It is developed through meticulous attention to people, a true concern for others, and genuine caring. One of our interviewees who wishes to remain anonymous gave us a heartwarming example of this kind of caring. As she tells it, "Unbeknownst to the troops, we had an employee here who was financially strapped so he could not afford to buy the kind of clothes we would like to have people wear at the office. I took him over to the side one day and told him that if he'd talk it over with his wife, I'd take him shopping. We went out and bought him new clothes, which I paid for out of my own pocket. No one here knows about it. The next day he came to work and was proud as a peacock."

Finally, the third component, a voracious appetite for *Learning,* is the primary vehicle for developing both *Business Savvy* and *People Wizardry.* Beyond its obvious utilitarian function, learning, both formally and informally, is a joy and a passion. Janice Jones epitomizes the thirst for knowledge we saw. This Ph.D. in psychology used her wits to build a highly successful venture management company. When we met her, she was reading *American Caesar,* the biography of General Douglas MacArthur. Janice explained her intrigue with this book by saying, "MacArthur was outnumbered by the Japanese 200 or 300 to 1 and he still won the war!" She applies his battle strategies in World War II to business in 1986. Janice doesn't learn only from books. She also learns from her business experiences. As she testifies, "I'm getting even brighter now. I don't mean that presumptuously but the more deals I put together, the better I get all the time."

All three skills just illustrated are essential for making you an astute and successful business person. By the time you finish this chapter, we expect you to pick up some concrete techniques and strategies to be more shrewd in business dealings, more adept at dealing with people, and more creative in extracting the learning from every situation. The first skill in the triad focuses on clever, creative approaches to business dealings.

BUSINESS SAVVY: BOTTOM-LINE SHREWDNESS

"No matter how great the power of the intellect, you're still going to have to persuade someone else."

SHIRLEY HUFSTEDLER

Bottom-line financial competence is to be expected among these successful women. Whether they are political leaders working with massive budgets, entrepreneurs writing business plans to seek capital for new start-ups, or corporate leaders interpreting profit and loss sheets, their financial acumen is apparent. They wouldn't be successful without it and many of them advise women to get this kind of knowledge. Not everyone has, or even needs, an MBA, but if you are going to be successful in the marketplace you need to acquire basic financial competence. However, that's not enough. *Business Savvy* depends on more than skills with budgets, mergers, and acquisitions. *Business Savvy* is a way of thinking. It is cleverness in creating show-stopping strategies that get results. It is shrewdness in diligently sticking to plans until it's smart not to. Finally, it is the adroitness of a natural-born salesperson in presenting the benefits of an issue or product in terms the other person can't (or never would) refuse.

We'll show you what this clever thinking looks like. But don't expect a front-door approach. You won't get it from Gail Winslow, who is vice chairman of Ferris & Co., a Washington, D.C., investment firm. She didn't start at the top back in 1956. With no shorthand or typing skills, she was hired as a girl Friday. At that time this young, divorced mother of two was simply looking for a way to bide time until something better came along. But when she got to Ferris & Co., that all changed. She took one look around and decided that she was going back to school to get her broker's license. Gail accomplished that feat within six months. Instead of fanfare, parties, and balloons to celebrate her achievement, Gail got the big zero. No announcement was made of her accomplishment nor was a promotion offered.

Gail's goal was to get out of the secretarial niche into a financial one with opportunity to grow within the company. Experience had taught her that straightforward requests from women didn't always get the best results, so she designed a clever plan. She resolutely came in one morning and gathered four packing boxes. This resourceful woman put them right in the middle of the floor, covered by a desk blotter. An upside-down wastebasket became her chair. When the powers that be came in that morning and saw Gail amid her new office furniture, they got the message. She got her real desk, a new job, and she was on her way to the top.

Julia Walsh used this same kind of clever thinking in 1957 when she was widowed and left with four young sons, eleven months through seven years. Julia knew she had to go to work, but she needed help taking care of the kids and didn't have the money to pay for it. Her brainstorming generated a clever solution that worked. She invited her mother-in-law to come to Washington to help her out.

What's so clever about that? Wait, the best is yet to come.

Julia made her mother-in-law a tantalizing offer. She asked her to become her business partner in an unique arrangement. Mrs. Montgomery would run the household and Julia would give her 20 percent of everything she made after taxes. That was not a lot of money in the mid-fifties when Julia was just starting out, but it became so later when Julia made it big. She also gave her mother-in-law a pension, health benefits, profit sharing, and a vacation with pay. The result was good for everybody—a prosperous Julia, an immaculate house, well cared for children, and a housekeeper-grandmother who was paid what she was worth. Even when Julia remarried and Mrs. Montgomery retired, she was set up as a consultant to the business and helped out until she died in 1969.

This kind of clever thinking and shrewd strategizing may be second nature for some, but for many of us it has to be cultivated. For starters, when faced with an obstacle, don't grab the first solution you come up with. It will probably be a very predictable, logical one. Nudge yourself to be a little outrageous as you consider numerous courses of action. Particularly in the early stages of your creativity, the more bizarre your thinking is, the better. Realize that these kinds of unconventional strategies are risky. They may surprise, even shock, people. But that is their advantage. They get attention and quite frequently, results.

Besides the shrewdness Gail and Julia showed, *Business Savvy* shows itself in another way. Over and over again when asked about what quality makes them successful, these women replied, "flexibility." While they are clear and decisive, they also know when to make mid-course corrections. When something is not working, they change strategies. The astuteness comes in the sense of timing. They don't prematurely abandon an approach, neither do they hang on too long. Unfortunately, there is no formula that can tell you the right moment to jump ship. Only experience fine tunes your timing radar.

A sterling example of this flexibility can be seen in a story

from Colombe Nicholas, a story that is apt to provoke contro-
versy. Now the president of Christian Dior New York,
Colombe was then the cosmetic buyer at Bloomingdale's. She
had been there only a few months and her experience up to
that time was primarily in retail merchandising. In this new
job, it was her duty to manage the activities of a construction
crew making alterations. Less than excited about this task, she
tried desperately to be exempted from this responsibility on
the basis that she ". . . knew nothing of reading blueprints or
the difference between a wet column and a dry wall." Management showed their sympathy by giving her a quick course in
blueprint reading.

Colombe arrived at her first meeting wearing a hard hat and
sat down with the union rep, a shop steward, and the crew
boss to lay out a work schedule for the tough deadlines ahead.
Colombe says she followed her long time policy ". . . to be all
business for the first few minutes of any meeting that involves
a new situation. So I marched in with a sober expression and
scrolls of blueprints under my arm, looking as much as possible like a knowing contractor. I sat down and began to spread
out the plans on the table, at which point the crew boss
reached over, pinched my cheek, and said, 'You're cute.' "

The image Colombe was trying to project crumbled. She felt
desperate and hopeless and was at a loss for how to proceed.
What she did was hide her face in her arms, and in her most
imploring voice asked, "Fellows, what are we going to do?"
The three men came to her rescue. It took them about twenty
minutes to find a way to meet the tight schedule for which she
was responsible. Colombe left that meeting feeling both subdued and elated. She was subdued because her plea for help
seemed an inappropriate way for a professional woman to behave. But, the adaptable Colombe was elated because it
worked.

As she sorted through the experience, she at first chastised
herself for acting like a little girl when she was treated like

one. But after reevaluating what happened, she decided what she had done was fine. Her job was to get people working together in an effective and amicable way in order to accomplish a specific task. Looked at in those terms, she had done a very good job.

Situations like this one are so difficult and controversial because they involve a judgment call about an emotionally laden issue. Colombe's "damsel in distress" response may not always be the right strategy. In this case though, it seems a frontal assault would have been much less effective.

Colombe's story raises some important questions that you can apply to your own difficult situations. First, do you have a plan of attack when you approach a situation? Second, when you see your plan not working, are you honest enough to admit it and smart enough to abandon it? Third, are you quick enough on your feet to try something new, on the spot? Fourth, what ethical considerations shape your choices of behavior?

Colombe felt ambivalent and questioned whether the ends justified the means. Ultimately for her they did: her strategy gained her the respect of the male construction workers. Had she attempted to argue or berate them, she might still be waiting for that respect—as well as for the work to get done.

Henrietta Holsman can testify to the effectiveness of Colombe's approach. As one of few women in a male-dominated industry, she has been exposed to male chauvinism. As a result of many experiences she advises a flexible strategy similar to Colombe's. As president of Stockton Wire, Henrietta has faced comments like, "Honey, what do you know?" and "You're such a cute little thing." She has weathered all of those comments and gone on to earn a great deal of respect and affection from her male counterparts. Here is Henrietta's strategy. When she faces discrimination, first she's charming, then she's nice, and finally she's firm and clear. What she isn't is combative. She believes that response only reinforces negative perceptions. That's not to say she doesn't know when to take a stand. But she's charming first because it defuses resistance and disarms people. Then she's nice because that allows her to develop rapport. Finally, as relationships develop and defenses are down, she's firm and clear. Both Henrietta and Colombe understand that people who are threatened would rather fight than switch and that men will be less resistant if women work with them rather than against them.

Being flexible and using clever, shrewd tactics doesn't minimize the need for the direct approach, though. That's where sales ability, the third part of *Business Savvy,* comes in. These women can sell the proverbial ice to Eskimos and they do it by remembering the key consideration in selling. They position their pitch based on what's in it for the other party. This means understanding the buyer's needs and seeing it from the buyer's perspective. Positioning is as important when selling ideas as it is when selling products. The common sense behind this approach makes it seem profoundly simple. But it isn't. Most of us are so hell-bent on getting our own way that we forget to consider what the other person wants or needs. Astute business people know you don't make a "sale" until you make the benefits to the other person paramount.

The most endearing example of this strategy came from one of our interviewees whose promotion meant a move to Southern California. She knew her biggest stumbling block would not be her husband, but her two sons. In breaking the news to them, she started out by saying, "You've heard of Disneyland, well . . ." When she came home later that night, they were busily packing.

> "I knew if I helped enough people get what they want, I'd get what I want."
>
> MARY KAY ASH

Donna Goya, vice president of personnel at Levi-Strauss, used the same approach with a work-related problem. She needed to go on half-time when her children were young but she feared she might meet resistance from top management. Her business acumen told her that a case pled on the basis of justice, compassion, and decency would be a weak one (although Levi-Strauss has the reputation of being an extremely humane employer). Instead, she did her homework before ever taking the request to her boss. This enabled her to go in with a plan that emphasized the benefits to the company and the boss, not her desire to stay home with her children.

There were a couple of steps involved. In lining up her replacements and redistributing assignments, she recruited staff members by showing them how the extra responsibilities would give them additional experience, new skills, and increased promotability. Then she won her boss over by showing him that Levi-Strauss would gain employee time and motivation from the change. Further, the logistics of reorganizing had already been done and the loose ends tied up. It was an offer her boss was too smart to refuse. Donna's desire for time at home was satisfied, but it wasn't mentioned as a consideration to anyone she tried to influence. Their benefits got all the attention.

Both these women got takers because they highlighted benefits the other person valued. Think about ideas you'd like to sell and people you'd like to influence. Change your mental set from what *you want* to what *they need*. What's in it for your boss to give you a promotion or a raise? What's in it for your kids to clean their rooms if they aren't bothered by the mess? If your subordinates are already feeling overworked and underpaid, what's in it for them to assume extra responsibility?

In all three cases, don't expect results until you can answer these questions through the eyes of your boss, your child, and your subordinate. That's what positioning is all about. It is the essence of having influence and shaping other people's responses to get more of what you want in life. It is also a fundamental element of *Business Savvy.*

A Potpourri of Business Savvy Strategies

"Stop volunteering time and start making money so you can turn around and donate it."

JANICE JONES

Shrewd thinking and clever strategies are the essence of *Business Savvy.* Here are ingenious tricks from some of the 100 practical magicians. Use them and get results.

1. *Take a partner.* Irene Cohen, president of Irene Cohen Personnel Services, has instituted this program in her personnel agency. No manager can make a decision without using another manager as a sounding board. You, too, can make use of a buddy system to check out your perceptions, ideas, or decisions.

2. *Gracefully exit.* Phyllis Kaminsky, director of the United Nations Information Centre, gives a strategy for leaving high powered meetings with male executives when the school calls about emergencies with her child. What she never tells those at her meeting is that her son is hurt because that would change the way they view her and perhaps diminish her credibility. What she does tell them is that she's been called away and will do her presentation later or mail it to them. The message for you? Explain your responsibilities and commitments in language that is acceptable in business.

3. *Joint venture with a man.* When Linda Alvarado, president of Alvarado Construction, was new in the construction industry and trying to establish a track record, she engaged in a joint venture with an elderly white-haired man. In this case, she gained credibility by association. You are judged by the company you keep, so hook up with people that add to, not detract from, your reputation.

4. *Avoid getting slotted in the pink-collar ghetto.* In establishing her career in advertising, Sandra Meyer, currently executive director at Russell Reynolds Associates, made a conscious decision not to work with the stereotypical "female jobs" in what she calls the "girdles and war paint" accounts. By not working with cosmetic and foundation manufacturers as was expected of women in advertising, she helped change stereotypes and distinguished herself by working with male-dominated industries. Put yourself in a place where you'll stand out and don't buy into limiting expectations.

5. *Barter.* As president of Hunter College, Donna Shalala has clear goals. So do her department chairs and theirs are not always the same as hers. But she's willing to trade. The deals work for everybody. In one instance, the science lab got renovation money and Donna got a science faculty that is no longer all-white male. Make your business life a swap meet. Look for creative ways to make trades.

6. *Neutralize the negative.* Jean Sisco, partner in Sisco Associates, advises capitalizing on people's strengths in such a way that weaknesses become less of a focus. She cites the case of an employee whose constant complaining made him the bane of other staff members' existence. More disturbingly, he was a

time-consuming and unproductive topic of conversation. His saving grace was a rare talent—a beautiful voice for making announcements. This positive trait was what Jean chose to emphasize, not his irritating habits. In doing so, Jean got his best efforts. Applause, not boos, pays big dividends.

7. *Don't devalue your experience.* California state senator Diane Watson wants women to maximize rather than discount their experiences. She would especially like volunteers in organizations like the PTA to recognize that a budget, is a budget, is a budget. She suggests the only difference between juggling the complex finances of a state government and those of a neighborhood school is a few zeros. Further, when applying for jobs, she advises women to highlight and embellish their volunteer activities. Don't devalue your experiences or sell yourself short.

8. *Stay grounded in reality.* Marjorie Deane, who publishes the Tobe report, a fashion forecaster for major retailers, requires her employees to shop retail for their own clothes. With their contacts in the fashion industry, they could easily buy wholesale. However, Marjorie realizes that the loss of empathy with the consumer would not compensate for the gain they'd realize in their pockets. Don't lose touch with your clientele.

9. *Grab the clues where you can.* For Shirley Hufstedler, former circuit court judge and cabinet member, this meant playing dominoes, cards, and chess after lunch with some of her brethren on the bench. She used the competitive game environment to learn how these individuals think and deal with stress. An added benefit of this socializing was that it built relation-

ships she was able to call upon when she needed help. Create situations where you can see other sides of people.

10. *Hire motivated people.* Patti Mancini, vice president at Rockwell, who deals with motivating employees, says she discovered the key to motivation. Don't expect to make a slug into a go-getter. Hire people who are already motivated. Then maintain an environment where they can flourish. Don't try to make people over. Surround yourself with the best and create an environment where they want to stick around.

11. *Roll up your sleeves.* Arlene Meeker, who heads Grover Manufacturing Corp., a hydraulic pump maker, won the hearts and minds of her employees when she spent two weeks on the production floor. Not only did she do almost every job in the plant, she developed rapport with her staff. Know your business from top to bottom and be willing to work shoulder to shoulder with people.

12. *Court the secretary.* Barbara Casey, head of her own PR firm in Malibu, spends as much time building relationships with the secretaries as she does with the clients themselves. At holidays, they, rather than their bosses, are the recipients of Barbara's gifts. They become Barbara's allies. When she calls to talk to a client, she always gets the "weather report" from the secretary. If the boss is gloomy or stormy, Barbara says, "I didn't call." You never know who can help you. Treat everybody with dignity and respect.

13. *Be Your Own P.R. Agent.* Pat Russell, Los Angeles City Council president, advises not to get so lost in doing a good job

that you forget to let other people know of your accomplishments. Overcome your modesty, socialization, and shyness. Proclaiming your strengths and calling attention to your successes is not conceited but it *is* savvy.

14. *Make phone dates.* Sally Berger, vice president of HBO & Co., knows how much time is wasted by busy people playing "catch me if you can" by telephone so she makes appointments for all her important phone calls. Minimize the opportunity for wasting time, maximize the opportunity for results.

15. *Alleviate anxiety.* Rena Bartos, J. Walter Thompson advertising executive, realizes that when people resist, it's because they're anxious. She had the job of creating the ad campaign for Pan Am when the 747's first came out. Her research showed that people were intimidated by the size of the plane so her commercials reassured passengers by bringing these behemoths down to human scale. The resulting commercial featured a stewardess taking her grandmother through the plane; the galley was called a kitchen and the ample number of restrooms was stressed. Emphasize the familiar to mitigate resistance when you meet it.

16. *Call it a pilot.* Sally Behn, currently president of Ferris & Co., says that often when she tries something new she labels it a pilot. This is an especially helpful strategy when the results turn out to be less than glorious. Labeling the venture a pilot takes the stigma of failure away from the outcome and legitimizes it as a learning experience. Not fancy, just smart.

17. *Gain power by giving it away.* Barbara Corday, president of Columbia Pictures Television, prides herself on structuring a collaborative environment that she knows is essential for creativity. She also builds commitment by sharing the decision making with her staff. According to Andy Hill, one of her employees, Barbara says four words no male boss has ever said to him. "What do you think?" Remember this paradox of power. You get it by giving it away.

18. *Get the best of both worlds.* Ellen Gordon, president of the Tootsie Roll Industries, gets great results by mixing older, more experienced employees with young novices. Old-timers bring know-how and wisdom while the newcomers bring energy and vitality. The mix makes for creativity and productivity. Value differences and utilize them.

19. *Walk the tightrope.* Caroline Nahas, vice president of Korn/Ferry International, an executive search firm, advises women to carefully balance being a team player with seeking visibility. Both will make you promotable. It's important to be your own best advocate, it's also critical to be a loyal colleague. That means volunteering for special projects, sometimes as a committee of one. It also means pitching in when you won't get individual recognition. Be sensitive to when the time is right for each.

20. *Keep your feet on the ground, even if you're gazing at the stars.* Helen Galland, former CEO of Bonwit Teller, began her career as a salesperson with no idea of reaching the top. When asked about her "career plans," she says her only thought was to do her best at whatever she was doing at the time. Her strong advice is to concentrate on the job at hand. Make the

mark of excellence your signature and it will become your ticket to success.

As you can see, some of the cleverest strategies are the simplest. Though they are all doable and practical, they are also uncommon and shrewd. *Business Savvy* requires you to be one of these kinds of thinkers. As a woman, take heart. If statistics and stereotypes are right, you have the inside track. Feminine intuition is your ally and should be cultivated for its worth rather than disparaged. Don't sell this kind of lateral thinking short just because it's not grounded in numbers and logic. It works because it doubles your impact by drawing on both right and left brain skills. While we are not suggesting that it is unimportant to know about business plans and annual reports, we are saying that's not enough. The story with the happy, profitable ending will be written by flexible people who think creatively.

PEOPLE WIZARDRY: THE PIED PIPER EFFECT

"I will pay more for the ability to deal with people than for any other commodity under the sun, including sugar, wheat and flour."

JOHN D. ROCKEFELLER

John D. Rockefeller was no fool. He knew how to get maximum results. So do our people wizards. Colombe Nicholas, president of Christian Dior New York, says that "Success in the corporate world derives from the ability to develop sound working relationships with other people. At the managerial and executive level, much—perhaps most—of what we achieve grows out of the relationships we build." While what Colombe says makes good sense, conscious development of good people skills is not common practice. Because human beings are social creatures, we mistakenly think that the ability to communicate effectively is innate. It isn't. We do communicate, but we don't always do it well. The women we talked with do. They have an exterior charm and graciousness that is backed up by a profound caring and attention to people. More than that, they have a comfort with themselves that helps others feel comfortable in their presence.

We scrutinized, analyzed, and synthesized their people skills to test the stereotype that women are relationship-oriented and especially good with people. We wanted to see if social adeptness came in the chromosomes. While relationship building is not the exclusive domain of women, after talking with these 100, we see the genesis of the stereotype. In spite of their kaleidoscopic diversity, there was a genuine tone of charm and graciousness. From effervescent and gregarious to serene and composed, from boisterous and assertive to retiring and gentle, these people wizards run the gamut of personality styles. Many of the women we interviewed were dynamic and intense. We can imagine that they would have appealed to some of you and seemed overbearing to others. Some of you might have been drawn in by those who are quieter and more serene while others might have found your interest waning from their slower pace. Regardless of style, they all have a knack for dealing with people.

As we reflected on our time with them, the nagging question remained. What do these women do that makes them so exceptionally effective with people? The answer is as diverse as their idiosyncratic personalities. Yet, there is a core of observable behaviors that run throughout. These women make others feel comfortable, welcome, and validated. They do this with behaviors as deceptively simple as making eye contact, smiling, extending a hand, calling people by name, listening intently, and taking the initiative to start conversations.

People wizards get beyond themselves and their problems to attend to the needs of others. They make people whom they're talking to feel like the center of the universe. This kind of attention is a seductive force that draws people. For you, an intellectual understanding that effective people pay attention to others is not enough. There are frequently wide gaps between what we know and how we live. Using the skills of *People Wizardry* narrows that gap.

This is not to say that the women we talked with have a perfect batting record. They certainly don't. There are times they admit to being cranky, having their tempers flare, and their charm recede into the woodwork. But they know how to behave to get the most from people and even if they choose not to use these results-getting behaviors all the time, they can dust them off when they want to.

"Employees are the best PR."

CHRISTIE HEFNER

How do you develop this facility with people? Patti Mancini, vice president of communications at Rockwell, gave us some clues. Five minutes in her presence and you realize she has a true gift with people. Though they had never met, Patti walked into the interview calling Lee by name, showing a warmth many people reserve for long time friends. Her openness and down to earth manner gave Lee a glimmer of how Patti distinguishes herself from the literally thousands of people who work at Rockwell. When Lee asked Patti to discuss the reasons behind her rise to success, Patti's reply was, "It sounds too simple. I really care and it shows."

Patti gave an example of how people respond to this caring. Several years ago she was promoted and transferred to the El Segundo facility from Rockwell's Downey plant where the Apollo and the shuttle crew module were built. When she had occasion to return to Downey months after she had been transferred, she got a "homecoming" we might all fantasize about. From the patrolman at the gate to a task-oriented engineer, she got comments like, "I wish you were back here. You don't know how much we miss you," "Oh my God, we wish you were back. We really need you," "Do you think you'll ever come back," and "Things are just not the same with you gone. If things get done, it takes so much longer to do them."

Patti had the same effect on her own staff. One departing employee sent a note that said, in part, "I would also like to thank you for the years I worked for you. You made them exciting and yes, demanding. But they were rewarding and you gave me opportunity to grow and mature professionally. Thanks again for all you've done for me."

Part of why Patti makes such a mark with other people is that in the grand scheme of things, no detail is too small. She showed this masterfully when she orchestrated the visit of Queen Elizabeth and Prince Philip. Not only was the British entourage made to feel at home with British and American flags and brunch with tea, but the Queen was also photographed in a shuttle simulation complete with a British pallet on board. Did Patti's attention to detail have an impact? We think so. The Queen began her year-end speech to the country with reference to the shuttle simulation.

Patti doesn't only attend to details for the rich and famous. According to one of her colleagues, "She brought the human being, not just the hardware, into Space Operations at Downey." He goes on to explain that an organization as large as Rockwell is made up of a lot of "little stores," like a city within a city. Prior to Patti, much of the communication was what he called "strictly journalism"—all written. She brought people to people communication into the organization. She instituted a series of "President's Luncheons" as well as "Round Table Discussions" to improve vertical communication by bringing together employees from the level of janitor and engineer to company president. The benefits were many.

Problems were solved, accountability increased, and young talent recognized.

What makes people from the parking lot guard to the president of the company respond to Patti the way they do? She pays attention to people, calling them by name and treating each as if he or she were the only person in the room. In addition, while Patti never compromises on the end product, she has learned the art of compromise in dealing with people. You don't build relationships and commitment by always getting your own way. Above all, she rolls up her sleeves and pitches in. "I participate with them and I never ask them to do anything I wouldn't do."

Maryles Casto, founder of Casto Travel, practices impeccable people skills, too. Travel may be her business but people are her work. We visited Maryles in the office of Casto Travel, a travel agency for California's Silicon Valley high tech "microchippers." The fact that people are what make Maryles tick was obvious from her interactions with her staff. Contrary to the usual "when the cat's away, the mouse will play" attitude that permeates many places of business, Maryles' employees like it better when she's around. They tell her that when she is not there, work gets done with no problems, but it is just not the same. It's lonely. No one takes the same interest in them.

Maryles believes it is her role to provide the *soul* in her company. She pays a tremendous amount of attention to her people and she notices the details of their lives. From matchmaking to inquiring about sick children, she shows interest in the sometimes mundane events important to them. The emotional "care and feeding" of her employees is a source of joy. It is also fundamental to the commitment she gets from her staff and is passed on to the clients. That's why they keep coming back.

Maryles knows her charm is not enough to make a company profitable. She backs it up with policies that show her consideration for people. Her anti-burnout policy is both generous and farsighted. She tries to send employees on work-related trips at least four times a year. She also cross-utilizes them. That means they can do basically the same job at Santa Clara and at her other offices in San Francisco and Palo Alto. Maryles, the astute businesswomen, knows they get a better understanding of the business through this rotation. Maryles, the humanist, knows this change of scenery adds vitality and variety to the job. Her most visionary policy is still in the embryonic stages. She's considering offering sabbaticals to employees who have worked for her longer than four years. All of this attention to employees makes them feel good, trickles down to the clients, and lands in the till.

Patti and Maryles show us the importance of caring about and paying attention to people. How are your people skills? If you needed volunteers for a committee, would you be looking at a sea of empty chairs? Do your calls for help from your kids consistently fall on deaf ears? And, when you need to delegate, do you have a hard time coming up with likely candidates?

Without help and support from others, it's hard to be effective. Those who consistently get support and help are the people wizards who know how to make others feel important and valued. We would like you to feel validated by the effective interpersonal skills you've already mastered. We would also like you to grow by integrating new skills into your repertoire. Take a look at the following *People Wizardry* tips. Congratulate yourself for the ones you're already doing. Then target some from the list below for your improvement. You'll feel better for these successful efforts and so will those around you.

People Wizardry Tips

1. Make a conscientious effort to remember people's names and *use* them. It is astonishing that something as simple as

being called by name can make people feel so good. But it can
. . . and does. Those who do, stand out.

2. Take initiative in meeting people. Extend your hand heart-
ily (no dead fish handshakes allowed) and strike up conversations. If you're shy and reticent about taking the first step,
remember that the other person doesn't like rejection any better than you do. Besides, a warm greeting usually is not rejected.

3. Smile. It is welcoming and reassuring to the other person.
It also makes you appear more confident and inviting. Ask
yourself the $64,000 question. What is the worst thing that can
happen if you smile? People might not always smile back, but
think how good you feel when they do.

4. Show interest in other people. Ask genuine questions, not
perfunctory ones, where you don't care about the answer. You
don't want to pry and invade people's privacy. You do want to
ask questions that give them a chance to shine as they talk
about events or ideas important to them. Notice the details
about others and their lives and comment on them. No one
wants to be a cardboard cutout. Under the bright lights of
attention, even a dyed-in-the-wool cynic will bloom.

Showing care and paying attention to the details that count
in building relationships is an integral part of *People Wizardry*.
So is being helpful to others and helping yourself in the process. One of the best ways to do that is to form a vital, useful
network. Building the bridges that create an expanded resource pool is one of the talents these super-achievers have

mastered. For them, networking is more than a buzz word. It is taking action and making connections. It is offering support and opening doors. It is creating access and visibility. It is helping the best and the brightest find a place to let their stars shine.

"If you have access to the top, use it."

MAUREEN KINDEL

From interviewing our thoroughbreds, we have learned that she who doesn't network loses out. By following their example, you can build a support base that connects you with qualified, competent people. Your network gives you a resource bank which provides access to professionals that serve as both a referral and a promotional system. Your payoff will be found in the opportunity to establish and maintain connections with stimulating people who aid you in opening new vistas, contacts, and ultimately, opportunities.

These savvy 100 do it better than anyone we know and the Hope diamond in this field of networking gems is Adrienne Hall, vice chairman of the board of the advertising firm, Eisaman, Johns and Law. She is not a household word like Mary Kay Ash, but among the 100 with whom we talked, Adrienne was the most mentioned and the best known. That's no accident. What she did to help us contact other potential interviewees is typical of how Adrienne helps people by connecting them to the proper resources. She functions like a clearinghouse, always making help available.

Here is a sample of how she "gives" herself to others. Advising that it is critical to build a power base in your community, Adrienne practices what she preaches. She is exceedingly active in the world of advertising, but she does not limit her extra-curricular time to that industry. She also serves on the boards of universities and is involved in local museums. She promotes groups for women of all ages from Girl Scouts and

YWCA to the Wonder Woman Foundation and the Downtown Women's Center for Los Angeles' homeless. If all that weren't enough, she creates Women's Forums that connect the most influential women within cities all across the country. This partial list of Adrienne's community involvement shows you the scope of her base.

How do you build the kind of contacts that give you the access and influence to open doors as Adrienne has done? First, you have to get over the mentality that using connections is exploitive and unethical. It is neither, as long as the use of connections is reciprocal and aboveboard. Having an "inside track" only gives you the chance to be in the running for the opportunity to prove yourself. Don't feel guilty about having someone open a door for you. You're still going to have to work your derriere off. Then once you get there you'll be in a position to extend a helping hand to someone else.

Next, you have to take the initiative to involve yourself in causes and organizations that reflect your values. You don't build a base like Adrienne did without putting in a tremendous amount of time. Only you can decide how much time and energy you are willing to commit to developing these contacts. Just realize that the reward will be proportionate to the time invested.

Creating Connections and Structuring Support

You may not have a bulging Rolodex yet, so here are nine practical ways to enlarge your network:

1. Take stock and periodically reassess your network. Your needs, priorities, values, and contacts may change. What is suitable and important at one time in your life may become obsolete at another. Be aware of the changes and adapt your network accordingly.

2. Keep a professional address book and update and weed out as necessary. Keep names and numbers of current contacts. Delete those from your portable address book with whom you have had no connection in a year. Saving old address books for a rainy day is not a bad idea, however.

3. Collect business cards and systematically file them in an accessible place. Write your reactions and notes on the back of the card to remind you of opportunities, your own personal reactions at the time of introduction, interesting points of conversation, and shared interests.

4. Follow up the initial meeting with contact such as phone calls, notes, or lunch. Take the initiative, show interest. All of us like to be on the receiving end of invitations and are complimented by another's genuine interest in us.

5. Keep yourself fresh in people's minds. Maintain contact with periodic notes, calls, or cards. Holidays are good times to reestablish contact.

6. Make it a challenge to add one or two new people to your network each month. Keep your antennae out and consciously make an effort to establish new contacts. Networks don't come ready made. They develop with conscious effort.

7. Increase contacts by belonging to professional organizations and attending workshops. This will put you in touch

with others who may have similar goals and interests. The benefits of extending yourself in new arenas are additional contacts, stimulation, and growth.

8. Compare notes and share resources and contacts with colleagues and peers. You have to give as well as take. Being a resource for others adds depth and dimension to your own life.

9. Remember to thank those who help you and give them positive feedback. Beware of being a user. Make as much effort to give help and support as you do to get it.

(These nine tips are reprinted from an article by the authors [March/April 1982] with permission from *The Executive Female,* publication of the National Association of Female Executives, New York.)

The beauty of these suggestions is that they are specific, practical, doable, and they work! There is no time like the present to get started.

LEARNING: FROM BOOKS AND FROM LIFE

We have a colleague, Alan Teller, who quips that everything in life is either for his entertainment or his education. He says, "If it isn't fun, I must be learning." The voracious learners we talked to share Alan's philosophy. They learn from all their experiences, the ones that feel good and the ones that don't. In fact, learning is often what makes them feel best. Some of their learning is formal. They read everything—books, journals, magazines, and when all else fails, they resort to milk cartons and toothpaste tubes. Their preference is for non-fiction. Some attend classes, take seminars, or get advanced degrees. And when their study is not in the hallowed halls of academia, they are busy being students of life. They continuously process their experiences and learn from both successes and failures, although they rarely use either of these words. Many viewed their accomplishments as the natural outgrowth of their passion rather than as an opportunity to take a bow. And they viewed their "failures" as mistakes that increased their knowledge and broadened their experience base.

As educators, it did our hearts good to see that learning was at the core value system of all 100. For them, learning has intrinsic merit. It brings them joy and stimulation while it adds beauty and wonderment to their world. Beyond being an end in itself, it also is a means of goal attainment. Let's look at the part formal learning plays in their accomplishments.

Formal Learning

"Without nutrition to the mind, the harvest will be bare."
SHIRLEY HUFSTEDLER

A liberal arts education gets the most votes as the best track to success in business and in life. While our interviewees value the importance of a strong business background, they cautioned against an education that's too narrow, weighted toward number crunching and high tech. According to most of the women, it simply doesn't give you the breadth of knowledge, conceptual framework, and appreciation of civilization that a liberal arts education does.

Not all the 100 have MBA's. Many are not college graduates and some didn't go to college at all. One is even a high school drop-out. Their formal education ranges from high school to Ph.D. and J.D. Not surprisingly, there were fewer college graduates among the older interviewees. Formal education was a less significant credential for women born in the 1920s and '30s. They know, however, that times have changed and they would be much harder pressed to accomplish their same results today without a degree. Of the many who do have letters after their names, some attended prestigious schools including Brown, Wellesley, Harvard, Stanford, Vassar, and Berkeley. But far more attended local colleges and universities in their own communities. We found that neither the level of education nor the institutions were differentiating factors in their achievement of success. Valuing knowledge and taking the initiative to get it—whether from a university, a seminar, or a book—were. This love of learning was planted very early.

California state senator Diane Watson's grandmother instilled that love in Diane and her other grandchildren. Senator Watson, who defines her business as education rather than politics, has gone from the classroom to the Board of Education and on to the capitol in Sacramento. But that journey began a long time ago when she and her siblings listened at her grandmother's knee as she read the newspaper to them daily. This was a command performance by Grandma. Senator Watson remembers that as a youngster, she heard Mahatma Gandhi's name so frequently she thought he was a member of the family. Between that ritual reading and an aunt who was the first black teacher in Los Angeles, Diane got the message. The way to a purposeful, rich life was through education. Now she derives meaning from passing that message on.

It's clear that Diane was influenced by adults who spent a lot of time nurturing her mind. If you had a learning history similar to hers, you are fortunate. If you didn't, it's never too late to start. Take those business courses you need and enroll in that humanities or art appreciation class you've been yearning for. Get a group of your favorite friends together and start your own study group. Tailor topics and format to your own needs and interests. We know one group of six professional women who start their week off with a breakfast get-together every Monday morning at seven-thirty. In this supportive and stimulating environment, they discuss a variety of personal and professional issues, drawing on each other's strengths and experiences. While it is enjoyable to learn with others, you can also learn a great deal on your own by subscribing to a publication that builds your mental prowess. Select one that will make you stretch in one of your areas of keen interest. Then intersperse the "tough stuff" with lighter recreational reading and other non-fiction.

You can also make a significant difference with your own children. What can you do as a parent to raise children who also love learning, especially if you're a working (or perhaps, overworking) parent? You can do what Diane's grandmother did. Give them concrete examples: Let your children see you read. You can also read to them or talk about current events at the dinner table. Even if you're not an avid reader, you can foster their curiosity by constructing "can hardly wait" rituals. Their most eagerly anticipated outings can be trips to libraries, bookstores, and museums. Their coziest memories could be of your reading to or with them at bedtime. And that's only the beginning. Experiences are portable. Bring them home. Make special times out of discussing the museum exhibit or popping that bowl of popcorn while you each read and then discuss your books together. These talks will work as well with first-graders reading *Care Bears* as with high-schoolers reading Shakespeare. You will shape the joy as well as the knowledge.

One of the most infectious characteristics, and the most potent in terms of awakening a sense of curiosity in your children, is your own sense of awe at the universe. This non-jaded feeling of wonder about life is positively captivating. Unfortunately, you can transmit it only if you have it and we're not sure how a person who doesn't have it can get it. One way to build your sense of wonderment is to do things with your children and see life through their eyes. We also have a suggestion for how you can foster it in your child. Build fanfare around their learning experiences, interests, and discoveries. Celebrate! From the first five-piece puzzles at age three to complex science projects in junior and senior high, there is constant opportunity to build skill, esteem, and mostly, the love of discovery.

Our next suggestion is not so easy: Retire your whistle and clipboard and give up your role as recreation director of your child's life. Children build resourcefulness and discover life when they are required to figure out how to entertain themselves. It's important for kids to be involved in constructive activities like music lessons, Little League, or the Scouts. It's also important for them to have discretionary time that they must decide how to use. As a loving parent who wants to give your children the best start in life, you might be tempted to fill their every moment with some structured, worthwhile activity. For working mothers, doing so is a tempting strategy to alleviate guilt. But in this case, less is more. Do not plan their every waking moment. Recognize that the more decisions (mistakes included) you allow them to make, the greater their learning, and eventually their survival skills, will be.

Informal Learning

For our interviewees, the official seat of learning is the University of Life. They see all their experiences as valuable lessons and they are able to transfer what they learn from one environment to another. One of the most delightful learners is Sister Magdalen Coughlin, president of Mount St. Mary's College in Los Angeles. While her mission in life is to help women achieve their potential through formal education, Sister Magdalen capitalized on informal learning as well.

She grew up in a small town in Washington where she learned very early what mattered in life. Working from the time she was eleven packing fruit, she found herself shoulder to shoulder with uneducated transients, women whom she calls some of the most marvelous people she's ever known. From their earthy realness she learned how to detect authenticity.

In fact, the entire milieu in her small Washington town was fertile ground for self-instruction. She didn't realize how fertile until she went to college several years later. When she encountered characters from the classics, she felt like they were old friends because she had already met their real life counterparts in her hometown. She sees nothing remarkable in her ability to use all of life as a natural educational experience. It is true that the act of transferring learning may not be astonishing, but the degree to which she does it is. We believe her compassion, depth, and wisdom have their roots in this facility to learn from the everyday experiences of life.

The work environment also presents plenty of learning opportunities as Jane Hurd found out. She shared an instructive tale of an on-the-job lesson. In her first job as a supervisor, she was challenged by one of her staff members. This old-timer proudly proclaimed that no other boss had ever been able to motivate him, and in his own inimitable way, he dared her to be the first. Loving challenge, Jane picked up the gauntlet and exhausted her bag of tricks and herself, attempting to light his fire. Nothing changed. Finally after much effort and sleepless nights, insight struck. Jane called him into her office one morning and told him she was through trying to motivate him because it wasn't her job. It was his responsibility to motivate himself and he'd better start if he wanted to stay on the job. Jane remembers that experience and uses the lessons from it to this day. She is currently CEO of one of the most progressive and innovative children's hospitals in the country with a staff whose fires don't need to be stoked. They burn brightly on their own.

Learning is the foundation of *Practical Magic*. Without it, there will be a low ceiling on your success. Learning allows you to develop the skills and formulate the strategies that make you effective with people and problems. What role does learning play in your life? Do you seek it actively? Do you put yourself in situations that stretch you and help you learn? Do

you seize the learning from serendipitous occurrences as well
as turn mistakes into lessons? If you don't, you're missing out
on two counts—the pleasurable and the practical. A good part
of the joy these women derive from life comes from their zesty
appetite for learning. Life is a daring, exciting adventure and
their continuous learning allows them to remain youthful,
adaptable, fresh, and exhilarated. Learning also gives them the
skills that make super-success possible.

Being alive means you will continue to have some win, lose,
and draw experiences. Even when your experiences are
"perfection personified," it's important to ask yourself what
you can learn from them that can help you in the future. We
believe that using this formula will help you extract the mar-
row from the bone of every learning experience and make
learning a constant part of your life.

Formula for Extracting Learning

1. *Acknowledge your success even in a "failure."* We remember
hearing about a wrestling coach who would greet his wrestlers
after each match and make them pat themselves on the back
for two things they did well, even when they lost. This positive
reinforcement was a ritual that preceded the necessary critique
of the performance.

2. *Analyze the experience.* What went well? What didn't?
Don't throw the baby out with the bathwater. Identify the
specific elements that worked and those that didn't. Discard
the latter.

3. *Play Monday morning quarterback.* Ask yourself what you
would do differently. How would you improve this undertaking if you were to repeat it? What single task, had it been

executed differently, would have made the most positive difference in the outcome?

4. *Transfer the learning*. It is this fourth step that creates the learning virtuoso. Ask yourself the "so what" question that leads to discovering where else you can use this learning. Find the next opportunity to put it into practice. Make a commitment to do something differently because of the experience you've just been through.

Practical Magic is essential for success. It is made up of tangible skills and techniques that are grounded in pragmatism and cleverness. For our interviewees, this behavior tends to be more of natural approach than a conscious strategy. It's been so developed and refined over time and experience that it's almost instinctive by now. Our thoroughbreds look at situations with a practical eye, whether it's a business deal, an interpersonal problem, or an everyday experience. They find the usefulness in everything, or they don't let it clutter their lives. Within them is a marriage of three parts. The first is the savvy business thinker who is continuously resourceful and lives by her wits. On this leg of the triangle lies her adaptability and her shrewdness. The second leg is home base to the charismatic people wizard whose genuine caring gets a loyal following. While she may conceptualize on a huge scale, she pays attention to microscopic details of people's lives—and they feel it. Finally, the triangle is completed by the student of life whose insatiable taste for learning forms her life's central underpinning. When these three facets, *Business Savvy, People Wizardry*, and *learning* come together, they create a brilliant performance. These women cast spells wherever they go, but unlike most sorcerers, they willingly exposed their secrets to us. Learn from their stories and you, too, will weave magic.

8
P.S.—PLEASANT SURPRISES

Achieving success is the subject of this book and the five factors you've just read about are tools that enable you to do just that. One of the curious things about success is that it seems so illusive. It's the proverbial pot at the rainbow's end—always chased, seldom caught. Yet the stories you've just glimpsed show that with hard work, success can be yours for the taking. This being the case, why is the opportunity to grab it often ignored? Shakespeare, who had an answer for most of human nature's eternal questions, also had an answer for this. "The fault, dear Brutus, is not in our stars, but in ourselves."

The fact is we are often our own worst enemies. People who could and should have more of what they want in life do not. They sabotage their own achievement, sometimes consciously, but more frequently unconsciously. Four highly destructive but insidious beliefs about success may be doing you in. The first is a fear of having to "sell out" in order to achieve. The second centers around the perception that successful people get "too big for their britches" and alienate their friends. The third involves the fear that the cost of success is the unraveling of our dearest relationships. Finally, there is the idea that achieving the brass ring is an arduous, joyless journey and that the ring itself is hollow. Quite the contrary. Our experiences indicate that you're in for some pleasant surprises.

We started our journey in pursuit of some truths. Finding out what it takes to succeed was only part of the quest. We also wanted to find out if these women had to sell their souls to get to the top. Had success gone to their heads? Is the upward climb a grim business and do they take their achievements and themselves too seriously? We are pleased to report that integrity is alive and well. Further, while confident and assertive, these successful, powerful women are refreshingly down to earth and unpretentious. They work hard at maintaining a strong base at home. Lastly, their journeys have been filled with laughter and joy.

This chapter will show you the guiding principals and ethics that influence their business dealings and their lives. In addition, you'll see the subtle distinction between confidence, which they do have, and arrogance, which they don't. You'll feel hopeful when you see the quality of the relationships they have with spouses and children. Finally, to your delight, you'll see how they use fun and laughter to give them a healthy perspective on life. You'll see that success can be achieved while maintaining integrity, a healthy ego, a happy home, and a sense of humor.

SOUL NOT FOR SALE

"Your integrity is one of the few things you own."

SUSAN BIRD

We've all heard the biblical saying, "For what is a man profited, if he shall gain the whole world, and lose his own soul?" We found 100 women who gained their corner of the world and kept their souls intact. They are true to their own values and respectful of others. There was nothing extraordinary about the principles they espoused. What is extraordinary is that they *live them*. Not only that, adherence to these principles didn't derail their success. Some apologized for advocating such trite and corny tenents as holding to the Golden Rule and having a clear conscience. Nevertheless, these are the principles by which they live.

This Above All . . .

"My integrity—that I do what I say, that I mean what I say, that I keep my word, that I live up to my promises—is all-abiding. Without this integrity, I have nothing."

DIANNE FEINSTEIN

They are true, not only to themselves, but to others. In our fast-paced and materialistic culture that values financial success and quick rise to the top, it is refreshing to see old-fashioned virtues like honesty and authenticity practiced and preached. These professional giants know that their reputations rest on their integrity, which they consider sacrosanct. They feel their success would be hollow if their dealings were dishonest or went against their moral code.

This code shows itself in statements like, "Treat the company's money as you do your own," "Never recommend anything to your clients you wouldn't do yourself," and "I never do anything I don't want to get caught doing." They have clear standards of right and wrong and they have the guts to behave accordingly, even in the face of life's temptations and pressures. Though lining up on the moral side of the issue is sometimes costly, they do it anyway. Here are a few examples of integrity on the job.

"Truth is smarter and more enjoyable than any alternative."

SALLY BEHN

Sandy Gooch, president of Mrs. Gooch's Natural Food Ranch Markets, refuses to sell foods with preservatives or additives. She bucked the advice of experts who told her that her business would not survive without making concessions to popular taste. Believing in promoting healthy products, Sandy steadfastly stuck to her guns and it has paid off. Her thriving company has just opened store number six.

Sandy's not alone in standing up for principles. Congresswoman Pat Schroeder fights for controversial legislation granting equal parental leaves for men as well as women. This challenger of the status quo advocates a position out of the mainstream, that men should have the same opportunity to nurture and parent as women currently do. Her stand does not endear her to big business or traditional voters. Though it could cost her votes in the conservative state of Colorado, this bold and outspoken leader won't compromise her views.

Another woman cut out of the same cloth is Phyllis Kaminsky. She had the courage to be honest with her potential boss, Javier Perez de Cuellar, the secretary general of the UN, when she went to New York to interview for her current position, Director of the United Nations Information Centre. She openly broached three thorny issues that could complicate an already politically sensitive post in this Third World, male-dominated bastion. She made a point of discussing her positions and biases as a woman, a Jew, and an American. With "three strikes against her," Phyllis still got the job, in part, because of her honesty.

A last but not least example involves Judith Runstad as a young summer law clerk. She demanded her client undertake a costly and time-consuming environmental impact study to get permits for a development project. This position meant Judith went toe to toe with a senior partner who wanted quick results for the client, not long, costly studies. Because she wouldn't back down, she became persona non grata, relegated to the "broom closet." However, when the Washington Supreme

Court made its decision to require environmental impact studies, she became the "ninety-day wonder" because her client, having completed that costly study, got the sole approval for development at that time. Judith now heads a thriving division in environmental law at that same Seattle firm.

In the end, maintaining integrity and refusing to take the path of least resistance did not impede the success of the four women just mentioned. Though they didn't know it at the outset, it helped create it. In any job, there will ultimately come a time when personal values will conflict with organizational goals or directives. The choices are not easy, nor are they always clear cut. Most of us want to make ethical decisions, yet choices are tough and consequences long-lasting. Inside, we feel the unresolved dilemmas with which we wrestle. What clues tell you when you go against your basic principles and fight with your integrity demons?

The loudest message will undoubtedly come from that wise ol' organism—your body. It might be in the form of headaches or backaches. It could be the recurrence of a chronic condition such as peptic ulcers or rashes. Whatever physical manifestations your conflicts produce, they will probably have non-physical companions.

Your unresolved moral dilemmas can also trigger an aggravated emotional state. Frequent outbreaks of anger or crying, lack of concentration or forgetfulness, are also some of the many signs that tell you when you are not true to yourself. While we encourage you to use others as sounding boards to talk over your resolution to ethical dilemmas, the best barometer of problems remains your own physical and emotional responses. The next time these symptoms signal that an issue is troubling you, pay attention. Spend time by yourself. Clarify the moral issues and get to the heart of the integrity question in each instance. Expect these dilemmas. They are part of business and part of life. You don't have to sacrifice integrity for success or vice versa. They can coexist. You also don't have to fight on every issue or try to right every wrong. There are even times when our interviewees would tell you it's important to compromise. But there are also those times when it is imperative to stand on principle . . . and they do.

Do Unto Others . . .

Hallelujah! In this highly technological computer age, the Golden Rule has not gone out of style. There is a popular misconception that to make it in business, you must leave your footprints on the backs of other people. What we saw in the upper echelons of achievement is that exploitation, haughtiness, and back stabbing are not the rungs on the ladder. It was nice to see people believing in the basic worth of every individual, treating both janitor and CEO with the same dignity.

Specific examples of Golden Rule behavior are hard to describe because this respectful treatment is ubiquitous among these women. Mary Kay Ash has based her entire business, and written a book on *Golden Rule Management.* You may remember that Patti Mancini instituted "Round Table Discussions" that flattened the pyramid at Rockwell. Employees at every level of that organization, especially at the bottom, were listened to and valued by people at the top. You may also remember the woman who gave her employee a professional wardrobe without taking away his dignity. There are ninety-seven others, who from our vantage point, treat others the way they would like to be treated.

Phyllis Kaminsky brings this Golden Rule attitude to the pomp and circumstance of the U.N. As director of the UN's Information Centre, her calendar looks like a "who's who" of international politics. Yet she always makes time to talk with young aspiring professionals. Phyllis can never refuse someone at least five minutes because she remembers being young and inexperienced herself and she knows how it feels to be treated decently, especially when you're just starting out. While her motive in treating people with dignity is altruistic, yours need not necessarily be. Golden Rule treatment also makes good sense in the marketplace because it brings repeat business. If that carrot weren't bonus enough, this sensitivity and thoughtfulness bring good treatment back to you.

CONFIDENCE, NOT ARROGANCE

"Some men have a false sense of dignity. They've never had to wash toilets. I can wash toilets and go into a board meeting and win."

HARRIET SHERBURNE

The second pleasant surprise is that these women, who are brimming with confidence and high self-esteem, are neither pretentious nor arrogant. Success has not gone to their heads. In fact, many questioned the perception that they are successful and, like newspaperwoman Mary Anne Dolan, caution against believing their own press. Using her own career as an example, Mary Anne parodies the success labels that are placed on her. In a circus barker's voice, she jests, "Here she is, ladies and gentlemen—the first woman ever in America to work herself to the top of a major metropolitan newspaper. The first lady editor, the woman talking dog." Mary Anne's tongue-in-cheek mockery of herself shows that she clearly remembers who she is, and that she doesn't take her position or her visibility too seriously. She acknowledges that when she is no longer editor or guest commentator on the David Brinkley show, she will still be "just Mary Anne Dolan." She has no patience for the pomp and pretense of power. Mary Anne, who knows the difference between arrogance and confidence, values the latter.

It's no secret that the confidence they demonstrate makes incredible achievements possible and is a critical ingredient for success. Judge Joan Dempsey Klein told us a powerful story that makes this point. Fresh out of law school and scared, she was confident about everything but her untested legal skills. She rode to work every day with a brilliant young lawyer working on more complex and exciting cases than she. He was a small man who was not particularly attractive. One day on the way to work he said to her, "Joan, if I had a little bit of your confidence, I could set the world on fire."

Not long after, this man committed suicide. In spite of his brilliance, he was wracked with self-doubt. The consequences of low self-esteem can be literally and figuratively deadly. We all have times of feeling underconfident but thankfully, these feelings don't normally produce such drastic results.

> "When you feel entitled, there's a certain level of competence and authority. You give out different signals. It never occurred to me that women wouldn't head these organizations."
>
> ADRIENNE HALL

Even confident people like Joan occasionally have doubts. She discussed hers. Before writing an opinion, she sometimes experiences an insecurity attack. "My God, what am I doing? I'm writing something that will have an impact on 20 million people. Am I mediocre? Do I really have the intelligence, the training, the judgment to make this decision? Maybe I'm in over my head." When this happens, Joan stops and compares herself with her brethren on the bench. Then she gets a very healthy perspective on her own ability.

Joan's strategy is a great one for working doubts through on your own. You can do this by analyzing how you stack up with the competition and by shrinking your superhuman expectations down to realistic proportions. But sometimes your perspective needs a boost that best comes from other people. Edy Fee got that kind of boost from her husband. When she went through a low period of feeling underconfident, he played a game with her. He asked her to rate the friends and colleagues she respected. This Avco executive rated most of them eight and a half on a ten-point scale. But when he told her to rate herself, in her eyes, she was a mediocre six and a half. Her husband asked, "Now why do you think these eight and a half's would want to associate with a six and a half?" His question helped her. When she got to work the next morning, in her cubicle, tacked on the wall at eye level was, "Think eight and a half."

None of us has the confidence to feel like a ten all the time. Even these champion self-esteemers don't. Expect some doubts. Everyone has them. We remember how surprised we were when Kathryn Klinger, president of Georgette Klinger Salons, told us that she sees some of the world's great beauties come through her doors and even they see their imperfections and find flaws in themselves. Their confidence gets shaken, too. No one is immune to self-doubt. But you can use the information from this self-doubt to produce a better performance, not paralysis. Take some action to bolster your confidence and start by proclaiming your strengths. This could mean asking for challenging assignments and telling those you ask why they'd be smart to select you. It might also mean acknowledging your own good work when you receive a compliment. Try a phrase like, "Thanks, I'm glad you noticed because I worked hard on this project." You might even nominate yourself for a job. That's what Ruth Rothstein did.

Never a shrinking violet in the confidence department, Ruth had worked her way up from lab tech to the president's assistant at Mount Sinai Medical Center in Chicago. When her boss left, she was asked to head the search committee to find his replacement. After a year of looking for a suitable candidate, the committee came up empty. Ruth took unprecedented action. Telling them that she knew more about the hospital than anyone, she proposed herself. She also told them if they didn't make her president, she would quit. She got the job. Shocked by Ruth's boldness? Are you inspired or intimidated? Some might view Ruth's behavior as arrogant. From Ruth's vantage point, she was objectively stating the facts and suggesting a viable alternative. The results speak for themselves. She has had a phenomenally successful tenure as CEO of Mount Sinai.

Where did Ruth and others like her get the confidence to take such bold action? First of all, they have a track record of achievement. It would be hard not to feel confident with the backlog of successes they have accrued. Equally important, they get support and validation from other people. In the majority of cases, parents were the primary self-esteem builders. They believed in their daughters. They told them that they were capable of achieving anything they set their minds to. As much was expected of them as of their sons. This high expectation and support builds healthy egos. Fathers were especially important during these formative years. Many fathers took their daughters under their wings and gave them business instruction at an early age. Many also shared a very special relationship and this instilled confidence.

Mary Anne Dolan tells a story about how a ritual with her father helped plant the seeds of her confidence. Every day he would come home from the office and sit in his big chair in the library. "He'd wait for me to come in and perform this little ritual where I'd sit on his lap. He would tickle me and ask, 'You are————?' I'd hide my eyes and giggle. Again, he'd ask, 'You are————?' and I'd giggle some more. After going through this litany several times, he'd whisper in my ear, 'THE BEST!' " As Mary Anne explains it, "best" was not a comparative standard. Rather, it was a message instilling the belief that she was loved for herself. It's easier to feel confident when you are raised by a family that believes in you and backs you up.

Mary Anne knows she was lucky to have this kind of familial support. Her answer to those who were not so fortunate is, "It's never too late. If we don't grow up with this validation, we can do it for ourselves at any age. Have a circle [of people] around that can do it for you." This means it's time to look at the people in your own life. What is their impact on your self-esteem? Do they give you affirmation? How 'bout honest feedback? And do they help you grow? If you want to increase your own confidence, keep adding people to your life who help you feel stronger and more powerful. Subtract those who don't.

FAMILY RELATIONSHIPS INTACT

The women we interviewed are masters at adding and subtracting, but in this case it's people not numbers that count. They build relationships in their lives with people who are nurturing and supporting and subtract those who would make them feel guilty for their success. Though they juggle priorities like all of us, they don't pay for their achievements by sacrificing their family life.

Relationships with Spouses

Many, like international management consultant, Jean Sisco, attribute much of their success to the strength of these relationships. She says she chose the right husband and the right career. Her husband Joe, former Undersecretary of State, does not mind grocery shopping, displaying gourmet cooking talents, and generally being helpful to Jean around the house. Of Joe she says, "He was always supportive and was never threatened by the fact that sometimes I earned more money than he or that I had my career first. He's been my best friend for thirty-two years."

This doesn't mean that there isn't tension in maintaining a

satisfying marriage and a successful career at the same time. Some of the women are divorced and a few talked about marriages cracking (or about to crack) under the weight of fragile male egos and competition. Only one interviewee out and out attributed the failure of a marriage to her exciting and demanding career. But others alluded to the strain of reaping more financial rewards and having more job satisfaction than their husbands.

While these women admit their success costs, career satisfaction and achievement need not unfairly shoulder the blame. Less successful people also have relationship problems and get divorced. The divorce rate among these women was no higher than the rest of society. Currently 64 percent are married or remarried and 13 percent are divorced. In fact, many of our interviewees mentioned their husbands as their best source of support, advice, and friendship.

One of the most touching examples of this support involves Barbara Corday, referred to in an L.A. *Times* article as "TV's Front Office Feminist," and her husband, Barney Rosenzweig. He is not only supportive, but grateful to Barbara for his increased sensitivity to discrimination against women. He tells this story in a recent issue of *Los Angeles* magazine. He took Barbara to see a movie, *Scent of a Woman,* in 1974. Everyone in the theater was having a good time except Barbara, whose knuckles were white. When he asked her if she was all right, she responded, "This is the ugliest, most sexist film I've ever seen in my life." Barney realized that something was going on that he didn't understand. "Since I'm Jewish, I decided to pretend that the women in the film were not women at all, but Jews. I was going to see if I would find this film offensive to my religion. Well, it was the most anti-Semitic hour I spent since viewing documentaries of the Holocaust." Consider Barney's consciousness raised and his support given.

The equality apparent in Barbara and Barney's relationship was noticeable among others as well. Gail Koff of Jacoby and

Meyers, Phyllis Kaminsky, director of the United Nations Information Centre, and Sylvia Drew Ivie, executive director of the National Health Law Program, find their husbands supportive enough to put up with the inconvenience of a commuter marriage. Gail's husband visits her once a week in Manhattan, and they spend weekends together at their home in upstate New York, and Phyllis' husband commutes on weekends from Johnstown, Pennsylvania, to Washington, D.C. Sylvia's husband took care of two small children and held down the home front when she worked in Washington, coming home to Los Angeles every third weekend. For most, there has been a way to work out the glitches in relationships both with husbands and kids. But it hasn't always been easy and they all do it differently. Like most people we know, their priorities constantly shift and the juggling act never stops.

Relationships with Children

Nowhere is the juggling act seen more clearly than in the relationships with their children. Sandra Meyer, executive director of Russell Reynolds, says, "I always felt it was a stupid question, 'What comes first, your job or your children?' It depends on the situation. If the kid is drowning, guess what? The kid comes first. If I have a major presentation and the child has a minor cold, the presentation comes first. You integrate it. Not everything is a first priority at the same time. You have to calibrate it."

Jane Evans, president of Monet Jewelers, is rare, even among our interviewees, in making no bones about the fact that work comes first. What does this mean to her and her family? For starters, it means getting up at 4:00 A.M. It also means spending a couple of nights a week in Manhattan, without her husband and son. This role model for other women desiring a corporate path (in fact, on her desk sits a trophy with a glazed dinner roll on a wooden base proclaiming Jane

"Roll Model") cites evidence from a Catalyst study that a CEO has never been a primary participant in child rearing. She, along with many of her peers, acknowledges the need not just for spousal support but for superb child care as well. Ten days after Jane had her son, she was back at work and she's had help ever since. This doesn't mean that she's abdicated her responsibility as a parent. The night before our interview was spent doing junior high school English homework with her son. It seems that the cliché "A woman's work is never done" is still true even when she's a formidable president.

These strong, independent women are creating more self-sufficient and less gender-bound children. One interviewee was not prepared for this outcome. Like many working mothers, this executive worried about the effects of her career on her children. After completing her MA, she decided not to work for a period. When she told her young son that she would be home every day and he wouldn't have to go to preschool, he surprised her. "Mom, not go to Montessori? They depend on me." Her guilt and concern were in vain.

This same woman was even less prepared for the response of her teenage son when she had a scare with lung problems. Quarantined at home because doctors suspected tuberculosis, she was relieved when the reports came back negative and she got the all clear to return to work. But she was not as relieved as her son who said, "Phew, I'm really glad. Mom, I don't think I could have stood it if you were home every day. We have lots of time together evenings, vacations, and weekends. I really like that. But I need my afternoons to myself." This independence frees them all.

Judy Rosener, the assistant dean of the Graduate School of Management at the University of California, Irvine, also believes in raising independent children. She makes an important distinction when she says she was always "super-mom." This mother of three said she was always there emotionally, but not in the details. Judy never made their lunches on the premise that she didn't know whether they wanted tuna, peanut butter, or egg. When her kids complained that other mothers made lunches, her silencing retort was, "Then you've got to eat what I decide, not what you want." Judy's son and two daughters sewed their own buttons on and knew that if they wanted to play sports they had to find a way to get to the playing fields. All these many years later, her son thanks her for making him self-sufficient.

They also show their children what's possible for women and like it or not, they have become role models. Kay Unger, the designer/vice president of the St. Gillian Group, tells the story of a family get-together with her brother, his wife, and their two children. Kay's oldest son, then a preschooler, asked his aunt Joan what kind of work she did. When she replied, "I don't," he asked with penetrating innocence, "What's wrong with you?" Out of the mouths of babes!

Mary Baim, the call-it-like-it-is president of Plywood Minnesota of Illinois, is joking on the square when she says one of the reasons she has a career is to show her daughter that a woman's role in life is more than just going to lunch. Does Mary take her role modeling seriously? We'd say so. Her contract stipulates that her eight-year-old daughter have a desk in Mary's office.

Role modeling, even by successful parents, cuts two ways. It is not always positive for the children. Parents' success can be inhibiting. When a mother casts the shadow of a giant, it can be difficult for her children to equal her achievement. Coca-Cola's "real thing," Barbara Corday, is president of Columbia Pictures Television. In that capacity she is the highest-ranking woman in the Coca-Cola Corporation, of which Columbia is a part. This co-creator with Barbara Avedon of the award-winning "Cagney and Lacey" understands that it is probably not easy to be her daughter. Evie's got a hell of a climb to surpass her mother's success. So do all the children of our interviewees.

Marilyn Lewis and her husband found this out the hard way. They had always planned that their two sons would join Hamburger Hamlet. Instead their sons opted for career paths that took them in different directions to avoid being in their parents' shadow. While this does not mean parents can or should squelch their own drive, it also demonstrates an often painful reality. As parents, even super-achieving, successful individuals do not have the power to mold their children's success in their own image. In fact, an article in *U.S. News & World Report* (January 1986) entitled "Ordinary Millionaires" reports that fewer than 10 percent of the children of self-made millionaires go into their parents' businesses, and that the parents are often disappointed in their children's lack of ambition.

Disappointment is not a one-way street. Some children's "you owe me" meters work overtime counting the hours they are not getting from their working moms. Kay Unger is a case in point. Recently she moved hell and high water to juggle her schedule so she could attend a party at her younger son's preschool. She had to leave early and when she asked her son that evening how the party was, he replied, "Mom, I pretended that you stayed." To make up for the time she doesn't have with them, Kay says when she's home, she's totally there.

Loving relationships matter to all of us even though they are sometimes difficult. They are no easier for these women than the rest of us, but they are no harder either.

LAUGHTER, THE CONSTANT MEDICINE

If someone had asked our prediction about what we'd see in these women before we interviewed them, we would have speculated that they would be driven and obsessed. What we didn't expect is that there would be so much laughter and fun in their lives. They see themselves and their work as important, not earth-shattering. They laugh at their predicaments and life's conundrums, but most charmingly, they laugh at themselves.

Humor and laughter are important stress alleviators in the pressure-filled lives they lead. Their hard work with long hours would make them right at home in Puritan country. But there is a major difference between them and the Puritans. To them, having fun is no sin. In fact, it is imperative—both in and out of work. It's what gives them perspective and keeps their lives from being grim. Problems are no longer the end of the world when you can laugh at them. Humor breaks the tension of difficult situations and leaves in its place a lighter touch.

None of these women has had an easy ride. For most, it has been more like a roller coaster than a rocket. What has kept them sane through all the ups and downs is their humor. Nina Blanchard, whose gutsy humor surprised and tickled us, laughs at herself when she quips, "Women with no skills end up being entrepreneurs." This same woman who says, "I was a malcontent in the Girl Scouts" charmed us with stories that showed the humor she finds in small things. She recalled one Christmas when she went to a freight yard where Christmas trees are unloaded and auctioned. She ended up having such a good time in the frenzied bidding that she bid against herself.

Besides bringing joy to the moment, humor keeps Nina and her other ninety-nine colleagues from burning out. Laughter is their best medicine and in the high pressure world of work, it keeps them healthy and up-beat. Take a look at some of the quips that brought a smile to our faces.

Everyone brings joy to this office—some by entering and some by leaving.

Sign on Judy Rosener's office door

"Mistakes? I would have married later and divorced sooner. That would have allowed me to enjoy having two children instead of three." (The third "child" is her ex-husband.)

CLAIRE ROTHMAN

"I used to believe I could change everybody. I now believe half of them aren't worth the trouble."

MARY BAIM

"The fact that boys now know how to use a microwave is not my idea of a breakthrough."

SANDRA MEYER

"If I have to hear someone else's children on a trip, they might as well be my own."

MARJORIE DEANE

These pithy comments on life pepper their conversations. Their witty and sometimes self-deprecating quips are disarming and endearing. For them, the spin-off of their humor is the fun and joy they create. Regardless of how high your aspirations or how far along the road to success you find yourself, laughter enriches the journey. It doesn't just feel good, it also keeps you physically, emotionally, and mentally healthy. However, we offer one caution in using humor. It has the potential to be hurtful when it is sarcastic and has a biting edge or when others are the butt of your comments. The reactions of others will tell you when you have overstepped your bounds and your humor has lost its fizz. Here are some ways to increase the presence of productive humor in your life.

1. *Fabricate fun and frolic.* You can do this by creating celebrations out of mundane events or special ones like Susan Hager's staff did when they threw a surprise fortieth birthday party for her complete with chauffeured limousine, champagne

brunch, and a birthday banner draped out of the office window. Surprise is part of fun that can lighten the environment and pave the way for humor.

2. *Put problems in perspective.* Humor is the great leveler when it points out the tempests in teapots we create. A University of Nebraska cardiologist, Robert Eliot (quoted in a June 6, 1983, *Time* magazine article) has a system for maintaining perspective. We use it often and it helps alleviate stress. Put these three little rules on your mirror, in your car, and on your calendar:

Rule number 1: Don't sweat the small stuff.

Rule number 2: It's ALL small stuff.

Rule number 3: When you can't fight and you can't flee, FLOW.

3. *Lace your life with laughter lovers.* Spend time with those who laugh. They will be among your healthiest, most enjoyable influences. Eliminate the witless wet blankets who siphon the joy out of situations. You can't afford them. The healthy soul needs lightness and joy. Humor-filled people can contribute that to your life.

It was delightful to find that you can achieve success while maintaining integrity, having fun enjoying a solid family life, and feeling good about yourself with feet firmly planted on the ground. It was even more heartening to see that the self-sabotaging beliefs about success were as real as a mirage. Realizing that the price of success need not be your soul, your friends, your family, nor your fun, frees you to pursue your dreams with abandon.

9
THE "SO WHAT" FOR YOU

We wouldn't be surprised if you had a number of different reactions as you've journeyed through this book. We certainly did as we went through 100 interviews. Perhaps your feelings matched the changing ones we experienced. When we began, we felt overshadowed by the extraordinary accomplishments of these women. It was as though a cloud hung over us—oppressive and gloomy. Little by little though, the clouds dissipated and by journey's end, the sun was shining brightly. If your feelings evolved from doubt to hope as ours did, you may see yourself in the following stages.

THE EVOLUTION FROM PESSIMISM TO POSSIBILITY

Stage 1: Defensiveness
Your first feeling might have been one of defensiveness. It's only natural to compare your own achievement with the Herculean accomplishments of these super-achievers. If you began to feel you didn't stack up, you might have either justified your

attainments and choices, or attacked theirs with thoughts like these:

—Who wants to be like these women anyway?
—Who knows what they're really like? They probably never have time for their kids or family.
—They've sacrificed everything for success. Their lives are empty.

This stage is a natural starting point in the evolution to hopefulness. If you got this far in the book, you probably went on to the next stage.

Stage 2: Depression

Once you've let your guard down enough to stop arguing with their success and making excuses, you may still be left feeling 1 down (or in this case, 100 down). This sinking feeling of inadequacy might be accompanied by thoughts like:

—How could I ever achieve what they have?
—I have little to show for my life compared with theirs.
—There is no way I can achieve on this scale.

How well we remember having these painful feelings of inadequacy. They were particularly acute as we talked with women in their late twenties and early thirties (a good decade our junior) who had significantly more to show for their lives than we did. We carried this low feeling of not measuring up through six months of interviews. It did not feel good. Thankfully, it didn't last.

Stage 3: Validation

Gradually our feelings evolved from depression to validation. We began to see that we also possessed the qualities we saw in our interviewees. They are driven, so are we. They love their work, so do we. They abhor excuses, so do we. We began to have thoughts like:

—They aren't so different from us after all.
—Maybe I'm a lot more like them than I thought.
—I have a lot of the same qualities they do.

This was the critical turning point in our evolution that set us on the road to our final stage.

Stage 4: Inspiration

Glorious blue sky! The sun breaks through. We were filled with the "I Can" feeling. This is the stage when, no matter what obstacles life throws you, you begin to sense it is within your control to make things happen. This feeling of personal power results in uplifting thoughts like:

—Look out world, here I come!
—I can do anything I want to.
—When I set my mind to something, there is nothing and nobody that can stop me.

APPLYING THE SUCCESS FACTORS TO ANY AREA OF LIFE

It took us a year and a half to go through these stages and evolve from our own doubts to a feeling of potency. It would be unrealistic to expect your evolution to be complete in the short time it takes to read this book. Nor is the path to possibilities and potency straightforward. But if you stick with them, these five success factors will serve as tickets and guides to achieving your own dreams. Not utilizing them can cost you, no matter what your role in life. The following questions show the effects of the five factors in various roles.

Manager

How effective a manager would you be if you . . .
- —weren't driven to do the job in top-notch fashion?
- —wouldn't work more than forty hours a week?
- —couldn't see possibilities for improving your department?
- —folded at the first "no" from upper management?
- —in spite of being a great technician, ran roughshod over your staff?

Entrepreneur

How successful an entrepreneur would you be if you . . .
- —weren't propelled by the desire to do it your own way?
- —didn't have the energy to sustain yourself through the trying times?
- —weren't willing to take the risk to venture out on your own?
- —weren't tenacious enough to approach the eleventh bank for a loan after ten had turned you down?
- —didn't learn from the inevitable mistakes you made?

Parent

How good a parent would you be if you . . .
- —didn't find raising emotionally, mentally, and physically healthy children one of life's most meaningful endeavors?
- —didn't bring joy and celebration to the mundane happenings of family life?
- —didn't show your children how to create options and maximize possibilities from their experiences?
- —didn't hold your children accountable for and teach them the consequences of their behavior?

—didn't teach them that from mistakes they get, not shame, but learning?

Career Professional

How far would you go as a career professional if you . . .
—were neither a change seeker nor a change adapter?
—found yourself being fragmented and distracted by doing too many things at once?
—didn't aspire to make a big impact in your field?
—couldn't bounce back from failure and disappointment?
—weren't good at selling your ideas to others?

Spouse

How good a spouse would you be if you . . .
—weren't able to adapt to changes in the relationship as both partners grew (sometimes very differently)?
—weren't willing to work hard at maintaining a harmonious and fulfilling relationship?
—didn't have the courage to confront when a problem was brewing?
—couldn't own up to your own part in relationship problems?
—couldn't sell your ideas to your mate by highlighting their benefits to him?

No one escapes the relevance of these five concepts. They can make you as successful as you want to be in life. If you are truly at the inspirational stage, you are through arguing the merits (or demerits) of these factors and are simply trying to make them work for you. These five factors are as potent as you'll allow them to be. They can be superficially bantered about between passing the bread and pouring the wine at business luncheons and dinners. However, if they remain all talk and no action, they will be hollow concepts. On the other hand, you can breathe life into them. If you use them as a clarion call to action, they can motivate you to achieve beyond what you ever thought was possible. Here are a few reminders for how to do just that.

1. FOUR-WHEEL DRIVEN—Find the source of your drive, then allow it to propel you. Whether challenge, change, freedom, or meaning is at the root of your motivation, take pride in your ambition.

2. MAGNIFICENT OBSESSION—Don't settle for a humdrum career or a nine-to-five job. Build your career around work that is a joy for you. Commit your energy and thinking without reservation to projects you love.

3. MEGAVISION—Challenge yourself to keep thinking bigger. Find possibilities beyond the obvious. Then take the risk to act boldly to make your megavisions megarealities.

4. NO EXCUSES, JUST RESULTS—Don't be stopped. Banish excuses from your thinking and your vocabulary. Continue to find ways to overcome obstacles and solve problems.

5. PRACTICAL MAGIC—Enroll in the University of Life. Take what you learn from every situation and individual, and put it into practice.

The proof is in the pudding. Two down and out consultants started on a journey several years ago. We were seeking universal truths that would help us lead richer, fuller, and more satisfying lives. Our quest helped us achieve that goal. If you asked us to capsule the most important learning we gained from our 100 role models on this incredible journey, it is that you can have anything you want to have and do anything you want to do if you just get out of your own way. We set our own roadblocks and limits. We also harbor our own potential for greatness. The only limits are the ones we place on ourselves. The world is waiting. We hope you are tired of waiting . . . to reach your potential, to see your dreams realized, and to enjoy the success you desire. All that you need in order to achieve your dreams is already inside you. You have what it takes. Now, go to it! YOU are the ANSWER at the back of this book!

PERSONAL ASSESSMENT QUESTIONNAIRE

	Almost Always	Often	Some-times	Almost Never
1. I am energetic and enthusiastic about my life and work.				
2. I avoid new situations and challenges.				
3. I want to rank with the greats in my field.				
4. I accept the consequences of my choices.				
5. I parlay each of my experiences into many opportunities.				
6. The goals I'm implementing are my own.				
7. I am a self-starter who is quick to take action when I know what I want.				
8. I'd like to be a big fish in a big pond.				
9. My "wishbone" is stronger than my "backbone."				
10. Reading is a priority for me.				
11. I commit "no holds barred" energy toward tasks that are important to me.				
12. I expect performance to be top-notch—both mine and others'.				
13. My goals and dreams are whale size.				
14. I am reluctant to continue when I'm told it can't be done.				
15. I present ideas so that people see what's in it for them.				
16. It's important to me to work no more than 40 hours a week.				
17. I continue to set challenging goals for myself.				
18. The feeling that "I can't" influences my behavior.				
19. Each person creates his or her own destiny.				
20. I resist new ideas once I've made up my mind.				
21. Work is a source of joy for me.				
22. I let things fall through the cracks.				
23. It's important to me to make my mark in the world.				
24. Discrimination against women holds me back.				
25. I am comfortable dealing with budgetary and financial matters.				
26. I get engrossed in my work and forget there's a world outside.				
27. I am happiest when I'm in charge.				
28. My motto is "The sky's the limit."				
29. My responsibilities to others keep me from working on my own goals.				
30. I have a cadre of people I can count on for help and support.				

PERSONAL ASSESSMENT QUESTIONNAIRE SCORE SHEET

Directions for Scoring:

	Almost Always	Often	Some- times	Almost Never
	1	2	3	4
	4	3	2	1

Score responses to items, 2, 9, 14, 16, 18, 20, 22, 24, 29 as follows:

Score all remaining items as follows:

Magnificent Obsession

1. _____
6. _____
11. _____
16. _____
21. _____
26. _____

Total = _____

4-Wheel Driven

2. _____
7. _____
12. _____
17. _____
22. _____
27. _____

Total = _____

Megavision

3. _____
8. _____
13. _____
18. _____
23. _____
28. _____

Total = _____

No Excuses, Just Results

4. _____
9. _____
14. _____
19. _____
24. _____
29. _____

Total = _____

Practical Magic

5. _____
10. _____
15. _____
20. _____
25. _____
30. _____

Total = _____

Grand Total = _____

Scoring the What It Takes Questionnaire

1. As indicated in the directions for scoring on page 197, score the nine items 2, 9, 14, 16, 18, 20, 22, 24, and 29 first. The rating for these items ranges from 1 point for "almost always" to 4 points for "almost never." For example, if you checked "almost always" on number 9, you would get a score of 1 point. If on number 18 you checked "sometimes," you would get 3 points.

2. All remaining items are scored in reverse, ranging from an "almost always" of 4 points to an "almost never" of 1 point. For example, if you checked "often" for number 1, you would score 3 points.

3. Transfer scores for all thirty items to the corresponding number on the Score Sheet. Total the scores for all of the five categories to come up with a grand total. You now have a score for each of the five success factors. The next step is to interpret what these numbers mean.

Interpreting Your Score

1. There are 120 possible points and a maximum of 24 points per category. The higher your point count, the more you have developed the five success factors.

2. Compare your scores in each of the five areas to see which are your greatest strengths and where you need the most work. For example, you may have scored 22 points on Magnificent Obsession and 16 points on Megavision. This would indicate that you love your work, but may be holding yourself back because you are not seeing enough possibilities or thinking big enough.

3. Beyond category scores, you can get more information by looking at items on which you scored 1 or 2 points. These would indicate specific weak spots where you can begin to take action. If, for example, you scored 1 point on item 10, "Reading is a priority for me," then you may need to start reading more and being more active in

pursuing learning. Or, if you scored 2 points on item 22, "I let things fall through the cracks," you may need to take steps to get organized. Consider some of the following: (a) attending a time management seminar; (b) buying a planner/organizer calendar; or (c) learning to delegate more efficiently, at home and at work.

4. Remember, however, that your score is subjective. It represents your perceptions of yourself. To validate these perceptions and get some helpful feedback, ask somebody else to take the questionnaire about you. Then compare their perceptions with yours. Focus on specific items where your scores differed. This is where feedback starts. Ask questions so that you understand the basis of their perceptions.

5. Once you've analyzed your questionnaire and talked about it with someone you trust and who knows you well, you're ready for the last step. This is where you transfer the insights from the questionnaire to your life. Look at the suggestions in each chapter and commit to some action steps that can help you further develop the success factors you need most.

APPENDIX: THE INTERVIEWEES

LINDA ALVARADO, president, Alvarado Construction, Inc.

MARY KAY ASH, chairman of the board, Mary Kay Cosmetics, Inc.

MARY BAIM, president, Plywood Minnesota of Illinois

BARBARA BALSER, executive vice president, Management Compensation Group, Southeast and formerly president, The Balser-Atlanta Agency

ERNESTA BALLARD BARNES, president and CEO, Pacific Celebration '89, formerly EPA administrator

MARILYN BARNEWALL, president, MacGruder Agency

RENA BARTOS, Vice President, Director of Communication Development, J. Walter Thompson

SALLY BEHN, president, Ferris and Company

SALLY BERGER, senior vice president, HBO & Company

BETSY BERKHEMER-CREDAIRE, president, Berkhemer and Kline, Inc.

SUSAN BIRD, president, S. W. Bird and Co., and President of the Committee of 200

NINA BLANCHARD, president, Nina Blanchard Enterprises, Inc.

RED BURNS, chairman, Interactive Telecommunications Program, New York University

FRANKIE CADWELL, CEO, Cadwell Davis Partners

BARBARA CASEY, Casey and Sayre, Inc.

MARYLES CASTO, president, Casto Travel

SHEILA CLUFF, founder and owner, The Oaks and The Palms

IRENE COHEN, president, Irene Cohen Personnel Services

KATHLEEN CONNELL, president, Connell and Associates, formerly vice president, Chemical Bank

BARBARA CORDAY, president, Columbia Pictures Television

SISTER MAGDALEN COUGHLIN, president, Mount St. Mary's College

ANN DANIEL, president, Winkler/Rich Productions, formerly vice president, ABC Television

BARBARA DAUM, president, North Seattle Community College

GRACE MONTANEZ DAVIS, deputy mayor, City of Los Angeles

MARJORIE DEANE, CEO, Tobe Associates, Inc.

MARY ANNE DOLAN, president MAD, Inc., formerly editor, Los Angeles *Herald Examiner*

ALEXIS ELIOPULOS, vice president and general manager, L'Ermitage

JANE EVANS, formerly president of Monet Jewelers, currently Director of Consumer Funds, Montgomery Securities

EDITH M. FEE, vice president, Avco Financial Services

DIANNE FEINSTEIN, mayor, City of San Francisco

JEAN FIRSTENBERG, director, American Film Institute

LYNDA FLUENT, president and CEO, Guaranty Bank of California

EILEEN FORD, Co-owner, Ford Models, Inc.

ELLEN FUTTER, president, Barnard College

HELEN GALLAND, president, Helen Galland Associates, formerly CEO Bonwit Teller

RABBI LAURA GELLER, director, Hillel Jewish Center, USC

SUE LING GIN, president, Flying Food Fare

SANDY GOOCH, president, Mrs. Gooch's Natural Food Ranch Markets

ELLEN GORDON, president and chief operating officer, Tootsie Roll Industries

DONNA GOYA, vice president, Levi-Strauss

SUSAN HAGER, president, Hager, Sharp and Abramson

ADRIENNE HALL, vice chairman of the board, Eisaman, Johns and Law

MARGARET HANSSON, CEO, M. S. Hansson, Inc.

CHRISTIE HEFNER, president and chief operating officer, Playboy Enterprises

HENRIETTA H. HOLSMAN, president, Stockton Wire Products

SHIRLEY HUFSTEDLER, partner, Hufstedler, Miller, Carlson and Beardsly, formerly Secretary of Education and circuit court judge

JANE HURD, CEO, Children's Hospital of Los Angeles

SYLVIA DREW IVIE, executive director, National Health Law Program

CONKY JOHNSTON, president, Johnston's Foods

JANICE JONES, president, Chartwell and Company

ANN KALMAN, vice president Media Services, CBS

PHYLLIS KAMINSKY, director, United Nations Information Centre

KATHY KEETON, president *OMNI* Magazine, vice chairman, Penthouse International

NANNERL O. KEOHANE, president, Wellesley College

MAUREEN KINDEL, president, Board of Public Works, Los Angeles

JOAN DEMPSEY KLEIN, presiding justice, California Court of Appeal

KATHRYN KLINGER, president, Georgette Klinger Salons

GAIL KOFF, founding partner, Jacoby and Meyers

DAVINA LANE, senior vice president, CIGNA

MARILYN LEWIS, chairman of the board, Hamburger Hamlet

PATTI F. MANCINI, vice president of Communications, Rockwell International Corp.

PATTY MATSON, vice president Corporate Communications, Cap Cities/ABC

ARLENE MEEKER, president and chairman of the board, Grover Manufacturing Corp.

SANDRA MEYER, executive director, Russell Reynolds Associates

MARTHA GONZALEZ MIKITA, vice president and controller, Corporate Accounting, MGM-UA Entertainment Co.

BARBARA MILLARD, chairman and CEO, IMS Associates, Inc., formerly president, Computerland Corporation

JUDY MILLER, vice president Marketing, Braun and Company

JUDI SHEPPARD MISSETT, president, Jazzercise, Inc.

CAROLE MORTON, president, Dylakor

BETTYE MARTIN MUSHAM, president and CEO, Gear, Inc.

CAROLINE W. NAHAS, vice president and partner, Korn/Ferry International

LANE NEMETH, president, Discovery Toys

PATRICIA NETTLESHIP, CEO, North Pacific Construction Management

COLOMBE NICHOLAS, president, Christian Dior New York

LARAE ORULLIAN, president and CEO, Women's Bank of North America

JOY PICUS, councilwoman, City of Los Angeles

DOROTHY ROBERTS, president and CEO, Echo Design Group

JUDY ROSENER, assistant dean, Graduate School of Management, University of California, Irvine

CLAIRE ROTHMAN, vice president and general manager, the Forum

RUTH ROTHSTEIN, president and CEO, Mount Sinai Hospital and Medical Center

JUDITH RUNSTAD, partner, Foster, Pepper and Riviera

PAT RUSSELL, president, Los Angeles City Council

BETSY SANDERS, vice president and general manager, Nordstrom

JUDITH SANS, president and CEO, Judith Sans International, Inc.

RUTH SCHARF, retired, formerly president, Ruth Scharf, Ltd.

PAT SCHROEDER, U.S. congresswoman, Colorado

FELICE SCHWARTZ, president, Catalyst

DONNA SHALALA, president, Hunter College

CAROL SHEPPARD, president and chairman of the board, Shop 'n Chek, Inc.

HARRIET SHERBURNE, vice president Development, Cornerstone Development Co.

MURIEL SIEBERT, president, Muriel Siebert & Co.

ELLEN SIGAL, CEO, Sigal Development

JEAN SISCO, partner, Sisco Associates

JULIA THOMAS, chairman and CEO, Bobrow/Thomas Associates

KAY UNGER, vice president, secretary, Treasurer, the St. Gillian Group

JULIA WALSH, managing director, Julia M. Walsh and Sons, a Division of Tucker Anthony and R. L. Day, formerly chairman, Julia M. Walsh and Sons

DIANE E. WATSON, state senator, State of California

ROBERTA WEINTRAUB, member and formerly president, Los Angeles Board of Education

JILL WINE-BANKS, deputy attorney general, state of Illinois

GAIL WINSLOW, Vice Chairman, Ferris & Co.

DEMOGRAPHIC
INFORMATION

Marital Status
- 15___Single
- 52___Married
- 8___Widowed
- 13___Divorced
- 12___Remarried

Children
- 30___None
- 70___Yes

Education
- 8___High School
- 21___Some college
- 27___BA or BS
- 11___MA, MS or MBA
- 10___Graduate Studies
- 9___Ph.D
- 10___J.D.
- 4___Other

Age
- 1___20–30
- 18___31–40
- 42___41–50
- 26___51–60
- 12___61–70
- 1___71+

Professional Category (some women qualify in more than one category)
- 65___CEO, Chairman of the Board, President or Vice President of a company or an institution
- 30___Entrepreneur, founder and owner of a business generating over five million dollars of business per year
- 12___Public Servant, elected or appointed to political office
- 30___Pioneer, one of the first women to break ground in a particular field